Love with Passion and Perspective
By Adele M. Lim
Published 2017 by Your Book Angel
Copyright © Adele M. Lim

All rights reserved. No part of this publication may be reproduced, stored in or introduced into a retrieval system, or transmitted in any form, or by any means (electronic, mechanical, photocopying, recording, or otherwise) without the prior written consent of the publisher.

This book is sold subject to the condition that it shall not, by way of trade or otherwise, be resold, hired out, or otherwise circulated without the publisher's prior consent in any form of binding or cover other than that in which it is published and without a similar condition including this condition being imposed on the subsequent purchaser.

Printed in the United States

Edited by Keidi Keating

ISBN: 978-0-9975727-8-0

LOVE WITH PASSION AND PERSPECTIVE

Pearls from a cross-border divorce
and the Hague Convention

BY ADELE M. LIM

PRAISE FOR LOVE WITH PASSION AND PERSPECTIVE

"The break-up of a family across national borders is intensely challenging, especially for the spouse who is the caregiver and financially dependent on the other spouse. This book provides a rare insight on the emotional and legal difficulties and complications of the experiences of the people going through this, and the shortcomings of the Hague Convention.

I have provided legal counselling and support for many women going through divorces. In my experience, most women rise to the challenge, to become stronger and better persons. Adele's work stands out as a stunning testimony of how one can not only move on after a difficult divorce but be transformed into a wise, compassionate, and loving being that has found her power and her peace."

— *Corinna Lim, Executive Director, AWARE Singapore*

"Adele's journey as an expat wife and mother navigating through international divorce yields great wisdom about the paradigm of relationships and the quality of love called upon to connect to one's own truth in every moment. Adele writes with authentic emotion, faced with a potential separation from her daughter overseas, and weighs her options carefully while holding the vision of the future she desires. By sharing her realizations, we are led to a place away from old paradigms of shame, guilt and victim/perpetrator, to an open space where love is possible no matter the situation."

— *Nigel Wylie, Co-Founder, The Resolution Co.*

"Adele has successfully managed to humanise a convention that has for years been the sword of Damocles hanging over trailing spouses living their life and dream in a foreign land. Several men and women have fallen victims to the twisted by-lanes of the Hague Convention. There have been several attempts made to change the basic premise of the Convention. This book appeals to the lawmakers to relook the Convention and make appropriate changes so that couples who are already working within fractured relationships can then go on to stem the damage that children have to endure, without getting caught within the cogs of laws that are mere words without a heart.

Adele's work at looking at separation, divorce, gaslighting, emotional trauma and the Convention is in itself a heart-breaking journey for many. So many individuals will identify with the words in every chapter and what's more, so many will walk away with the assurance that in this difficult journey, they are not alone. They may even learn to relook at their own journey and possibly find a middle road that is bereft of bitterness. Hopefully with change agents like Adele, one day this murky territory of separation and divorce will become easier to negotiate."

— *Sangeeta Nambiar, Theatre Director, Founder: Finally She Spoke*

"Vitally important to the health and wellbeing of our children. Laws that impede a parent's rights to enjoy a healthy relationship with their children damage the structure of all societies. Adele's compassionate and powerful presentation opens the path for resolution rather than revolution."

— *Dr. Mark E Pierce, Board Certified Internal Medicine*

"Feminist writers in decades past have been exploring the effect of socio-political meaning upon women's individual identity formation, as the core identity of women can be hemmed in and shaped by social values and beliefs – mainly others' beliefs of what our roles and our lives should be. So instead of achieving our core identity structure, many women found themselves operating with "The Divided Self" (Washington 1981) – compartmentalising our reality, our talents, our dreams, our individuality. When our roles become who we are, our identity tend to go submerged and hard to resurface through time.

This book is about that life-long universal search of who we are as women – to unleash the "Suspended or Submerged Self" by taking step to evolve the "Emergent Self." Adele, instead of shrinking back from tough life experiences, decided to use her struggle to step out to trust herself and others enough to disclose her experiences.

The book displayed a beautiful balance between the "Caring Self" and her "Agential Self." Her narrative of her own and others' stories show that caring without agency stifles us and our own development. However, she is sensitive enough to know that overuse of the Agential Self without care, and resentment will overtake healing. Adele, through this book, shows readers that her "suffering self" needs to go beyond having courage to express deep emotions, to seek resources within herself and her network for action and change in both the situation and relationship that stifle that deep growth. She uses her cognitive, rational, and emotional selves to move on.

Instead of allowing the conspiracy of isolation and silence that surround this type of situation, she connected with a larger community. She inquired, sought support, spoke, wrote, and shared her perspectives. Hence, by expanding her relational connection, she drew fresh energy to face the paradox of conflict, contradiction, caring and compassion of self and others.

This book has a solid content exposition of the Hague

Convention, which is useful to others who found themselves in similar situations. But more importantly, this book also serves as a reminder that the narratives we hold in a situation like this can be contradicted. Instead of living as if we have limited or no choices, staying powerless and feeling out of control, being overtaken by the desire to be potentially destructive to those who have done wrong to us, or overcome by stress, we can attempt at agential self-expression, to encourage others to rise above circumstances and to proactively create the situation we want.

I am sure different readers will get different nuggets of truth from this book – from knowing the implication of the Hague Convention, to how to live through this type of situation with potency, growth and agency."

— *Dr Mee Yan Cheung-Judge, Director of Quality-Equality. Ltd, Oxford UK, Dean of NTL Organisation Development Certificate (2006-2017) and Recipient of the Life time achievement award of Organisation Development Network in USA and IODA (International OD Association)*

"A brave and articulate body of work, Adele challenges us to cut through the human story of love, relationship and parenting in the context of international divorce and see through new eyes. Adele offers an expanded, yet grounded spiritual roadmap for traversing one of life's most heartfelt challenges. She is the voice of the Graceful Warrior, challenging us to live from a higher paradigm and expanded level of accountability – one that is in alignment with the next wave of our evolutionary development."

— *Kerri Chinner, BSW, Soul Coach, Facilitator, Shamanic and Energy Medicine Practitioner*

"A breakdown in any relationship tears the very fabric that one has become familiar with. A tear in a family relationship especially one as fundamental as one of husband and wife shakes the core of all other family relationships.

In the times we live in, oftentimes this also transcends oceans that divide us. As there are more cross-border marriages, cross cultural bonds, multi-lingual exchanges, cross jurisdictional issues and personal characters that divide us, people are ill-informed when the tear occurs. The instinct is to protect the ones we hold dear and ensure that the ones we love are not left behind.

People go straight into battle without having any thought to alternative journeys for dispute resolution, which allows parties to rediscover how to manage situations, deal with each other by making difficult conversations constructive and come to solutions themselves that are especially workable only for their family.

In her book, Adele has successfully reached out first to give a candid account and to share her own journey. Her honesty that is refreshing can only stem from one who has gained wisdom and insight in what was a difficult time.

The journey is not about who has won but whether one is able to rise to a new platform to continue be a better parent with each new day."

— *Helen Chia-Thomas, Founder at Trinity ADR Pte Ltd ... an exhilarated mother*

"A must-read, how-to guide for all expat cross border parents contemplating or already in the process of divorce. Adele Lim poetically captures and explores the delicate yet robust fabric of life, marriage and selfhood against the backdrop of relational conflict, breakdown and turmoil. Her book inspires and energises through her own truth-seeking momentum, vibrating experientially derived ideas to catalyse personal growth through her deep-dive analyses of the soul and psyche. This is a joyous deconstruction to be reflected on, enjoyed and ultimately to inform where there is little specific information relating to the practical, psychological and spiritual consequences of the Hague Convention. Most importantly, Adele reminds us that beyond information, procedure and process lies the promised

land of freedom, illuminated by the simple truth that we are always free if we can embrace fear and immerse ourselves in the perpetual light of love until it and us are one. Read this and it will change not just your life for the better but that of your child's and partners too."
— *Laurence Guinness, Chief Executive of The Childhood Trust, father, husband and lover of life*

"Adele Lim's Love with Passion and Perspective was both an easy and complicated read for me. Adele's writing is so fluid and it's so clear to see she writes from a place of passion, experience, and intention to provide support and education in matters of both legality of divorcing with children and the conscious heart space. Because of this, I found myself breezing through this book, absorbing her knowledge and nodding in agreement.

I found the reading difficult at times, purely in an emotional capacity; my family has been through the experience of Child Abduction and it was absolutely the most difficult experience we have ever been through. The Hague Convention was not argued in my family's case. Provisionally and idealistically, had it been, my family's balance would have been restored – yet this is a statement that is simply not true. What Adele shares, about "vibrating your dream," is truly the essence of being in heart space consciousness, walking this life with and in love. It is this notion that I agree, if both parents can practice loving kindness in their separation and consideration of their children, there will be a lot less damage done and children stepping into a new reality of what family life is, perhaps have the chance of a substantially decreased negative impact from these circumstances. It's time for a return to love and Adele's Love with Passion and Perspective is truly about parting with love the same way you came together with love."
— *Amanda Scully, independent business owner and former Managing Director of Digital Vandal*

"It is clear from reading Adele's book that when it comes to the issues of human marital interrelations, the International Law precedents made by the Hague Convention, leave a lot of both ethical and legal questions still unanswered that produce pain and suffering, stress, and disharmony. Cases are cited and the various realities presented whereby one gets the feeling that this law is a 'work in progress' that may not have been fully thought through, yet.

Adele's focus on the spiritual to penetrate the complexity of the situations she came across is laudable. Huge external, relatively immoveable forces, such as laws, unfairness, frustration, loss, grief and the conflicts of loyalties, emotional challenges, psychological puzzles and practical limits of immigration policies, served as tools to turn things around and emerge creative, resilient, and resourceful.

I was encouraged to find her focus developing towards healing and progress by removing the pain therapeutically and expanding into creative insight in harmony with Buddhist wisdom, rather than investing energy into analysing the root causes of every unique individual trauma that led to separation and divorce, yet recognising its needs by putting in just enough energy to engage interest and be an eye-opener. She reveals how one can emerge from the shock, anger, depression and bargaining with reality, to cope maturely with the grief and loss, progressing to an enlightened acceptance whereby light is shone where darkness remains. May many beings be freed from avoidable suffering thereby."

— *Bhante Ven Rakkhita Samanera (UK), Buddhist Monk*

"Having gone through the international divorce myself, complicated by the Hague Convention, I found the words used and feelings expressed in Adele's book bearing many similarities to my own experience. My divorce triggered a personal desire to look into the spiritual side more deeply in order to benefit from the complexity of the situation and I invested my energy into self-development, self-growth, and enlightenment so that I can share my personal experience with others and help women to remain strong and empowered during the toughest times in their lives.

It takes more than one's desire to break life-long habits of thinking and doing things; it is a whole new way of living that responds atypically to the stresses of divorce. Thus, a book like this is rare. It is a great tool for those going through divorce and who want to truly gain from the experience… for those who feel the urge to improve themselves by losing the typical victim role and fill themselves up with love and compassion. Read it. Click that switch on for the sake of your present and your future, bring that light of love within you back to life. With great respect and appreciation to Adele's work."

— *Irinka Vselennaya, social activist, law expert-volunteer, HR specialist, founder of Mothers United Movement International (MUMI)*

"Divorce. It's way more than just a word. It's failure. It's heartbreak. It's a reset. It's a legal minefield. It's conflict. It's chaos. It is also, according to Adele Lim, an opportunity. Tying in the complexities of a divorce, international child custody laws and the deeper questions this presents, she gives an account of extremely challenging events met with equally determined spiritual purpose. As marriages across borders and cultures become more common in our world, Adele Lim provides a story about the great difficulties when it doesn't work out, while continually informing us that these moments offer us the space and reflection to move forward to better places in our lives. A wonderful read, starkly relevant in today's world."

— *Paul Laurenson, behavioural expert and author of The Element of Surprise*

"Using immense self-reflection and professional, academic and personal research, Adele has shown amazing strength and future focus, enabling her path to become clear. Her understanding of consequences and visualising alternatives helped shape critical decisions that she needed to make. Accepting joint responsibility for behaviours and actions became paramount for her family unit's happiness regardless of (real or perceived) loss of ground. Handling guilt and forgiveness play a huge part in the healing process and Adele's book gives sincere guidance and advice based on how she coped with these intense feelings during her own journey."
— *Samantha Rich, HR Executive Director*

"Adele has written a fascinating book, which resonates and informs at a few levels. She intersperses all the stories, sharing how to bring more compassion and love into difficult situations, with a number of reminders on how to ensure that couples do their best to honour their children, even in challenging times. Bringing to light the limitations and flaws in the Hague Convention brings a systemic view to the book. With so many cross-border marriages in this global village we live in, it is key that the Convention is updated so families can be protected from abuse and entrapment, and live healthy lives."
— *Douglas O'Loughlin PhD, Organisation Development Consultant*

"It takes immense courage to open up about a difficult marriage and also take responsibility for having co-created that, making the relationship what it is. But Adele surmounted fears and barriers to bring this illuminating and heartfelt insight into what she learnt. Her storytelling is personable and relatable, and this book is filled with many invaluable lessons for singles or couples.

I feel encouraged that there are women like Adele who dare

to speak up, so that others may find strength to carve their own path and find happiness for themselves."
— *Yvonne Chan, News anchor and former management associate at HSBC Singapore and London*

"Rather than let a painful, stressful and ambiguous cross-border divorce harden her, Adele chose instead to face it with courage, letting the situation soften her, and, in the process, creating a roadmap for others to learn from. Throughout her book, Adele displays a powerful combination of self-awareness, wisdom and grace. Her constant focus on her vision of love and harmony where all parties of the divorce can grow and reach for their full potential, is truly inspiring."
— *Aneace Haddad, Executive Coach, Keynote Speaker, Culture Shifter*

"There are many moments in our life when some intuitive questions about work, relationship or health arises but we are too afraid to face our own shadows or simply not bothered to step deep into it, even though we all know that that is part of our light.

Adele is a beautiful, wise woman and mother who is capable of listening to her inner voice and take the risk to change her life for the better and protect her daughter at any time. Her wisdom, courage and stories are inspiring and uplifting for all women. We all thank Adele for sharing her gift."
— *Wakako Arimizu, Director of healthy raw sweets brand, Nashwa Bliss*

"An honest and courageous book on what happens when a cross border family breaks down.

Adele Lim shares her powerful account of navigating through a deteriorating relationship whilst on relocation. She explores sensitive and taboo relationship issues whilst also delving into the impact the Hague convention has on couples

who are separating and their children. Her perspective and positivity makes for an enlightening read, one that anyone who has relocated to be with loved ones will be able to relate to."
— *Shermaine Low, Information Technology Professional, wife, and mother*

"To quote from the book: 'Love seeks not weakness but to make us, independent. Love is not attachment but of pure perspective. When love loses its perspective it's not love. It has in it, fear.' This describes the complexity of relationship and how it evolves through time. A good resource that raises the awareness of broader implications when relationship evolves and decisions have to be made."
— *Jolene Teo, international career woman, wife, mother*

"I went through an international divorce myself a few years ago and a lot of questions were still unanswered. Reading Adele's book made me understand some particular situations better and it gave me more clarity on the whole process. I enjoyed reading the book and can only recommend it to women in similar situations."
— *Tatjana Richter, former trader, business owner and student of life*

For Earthwalk Issa... as you "anchor our next steps ahead which allows the work to be possible at all for the collective." Here it is to Love.

ACKNOWLEDGEMENTS

I am grateful to my ex-husband for all the experiences we shared as friends, as a dating couple, a married couple, a separating couple, a divorced couple and as a co-parenting team.

I am indebted to my parents and brother for being there to shelter and support when I most needed it.

I appreciate my editor and publisher Keidi Keating for finding me and shining her love and light on this piece of work.

I wish to express my gratitude to Hillary Munyoro for his contribution towards Part 2, and Dr. Nancy Sutton-Pierce for her contribution towards Part 3.

I wish to express special thanks to these individuals, named here in no special order, for their role in and meaningful contributions towards this project.

Sangeeta Nambiar, Amara Charles, Shyena Venice, Danielle Lee, Yvonne Chan, Monita Sen, Irina Miu, Anutosh Foo, Ellen Vanhoven, Pi Villaraza, Serena Olsen, Pamela Akasha Kaur, Wakako Arimizu, Ralf Schneider, Katie Hodgson, Alison Whybrow, Anne-Carole Chaumet, Ruby Tan, Heather Hagan, Yoshie Ruth Linton, Mee-Yan Cheung-Judge, Douglas O'Loughlin, Kerri Chinner, Volker Krohn, Vera Culkoff, Helen Jones, Ruth Lee, Ksenia Anikina, Judith Hemming, Anutosh Foo, Samantha Rich, Nicole Noe Chronell, Tatjana Richter, Jayme Cusack Joyce,

Jacqueline Renz, Tan Poh Li, Noviza Ramadhan, Helen Chia-Thomas, Corinna Lim, Sheryl Lim Madsen, Belle Chang Carrie, Isobel Dent, Amanda Scully, Nicole Yau, Jessica Harris, Aneace Haddad, Nigel Wylie, Roz Osborne, Catherine Rose-Yates, Irinka Vselennaya, Violet and Jason Hau.

Last but not least, I am grateful to receive all the resources I need on this journey and I appreciate my daughter for all that she is, the joy I experience with her, and the reminder of unconditional love that she brings to me by mirroring the pure, wise, gentle, strong, and all-inclusive, truth-honouring inner child.

Thank you!

FOREWORD

In the summer before my freshman year of high school, my two younger sisters, my mom, and I, quietly spent several weeks slowly packing. We were preparing to move – and we were planning to leave my father behind. Then, one day in midsummer, we did it. The moving truck took our large pieces of furniture and boxes, and the four of us got in the car. When my father returned home from work that evening, he came back to an empty house without word that we would not be there to greet him.

My father is an alcoholic with an aggressive personality and strong internal system of interpretation for how he views the world, including the rules he chooses to live by. My mother is narcissistic in nature with deeply rooted relational dependencies and personal insecurities. My sisters and I experienced many abuses and traumas growing up between two parents of conflicting perspectives, each of whom held both Victim and Perpetrator polarities in their shared dynamics. It was my middle sister and I who eventually sat down with my mom one day and sparked a catalyst for her separation from my father.

Even without the additional challenges of an international marriage, in relation to the Hague Convention coming between a parent and child, divorce is often a long and arduous process - especially when either or both parents are fighting to win something, whether it be love, custody, property, financial support, emotional wellbeing, or sanity. As a child of divorced parents, who also played the role of "little parent" for her mother, it was clear that my parents were better off independent than together – but could either of them ever truly exist as independents when something in their self-relationship held so tightly to dependency and guilt-based structures of engagement?

For anyone that personally holds narrative frameworks of divorce within their relationship structures, whether as a parent or child, seeing it as a challenge that is needed in order to build up reserves of energy required for evolution is a powerful reminder that part of us is always choosing our experiences. I see my past not as something to blame my parents for, nor victimize myself for having experienced, but as something I chose for my life path, even before I was born. I needed to be birthed to parents who would hold this contractual agreement with each other in order to evolve at a very early age through my direct relation to this process – as a child of abuse, neglect, violence, guilt, shame, fear, rejection, separation, and divorce, among the many. Mothers, fathers, sons, and daughters each must determine who they are, how they exist, and what conditions they will allow to be seeded within their own perspectives and systems of interpretation. This will either create momentum towards catalyzing change and evolution, or it will create the conditions by which one experiences great tensions between ego and consciousness. Whether a person breaks or becomes more supple and adaptable to life flow and trust might only be known by engaging fully in the processes as they are made visible and directly experienced while the narrative itself unfolds.

What I admire most about Adele is her constant ability to reflexively reflect on her journey through relationship, marriage, co-parenting, and divorce with a confidence that could only come from the heart. Her words insightfully speak of a deep resonance with Trust. To trust oneself is the second greatest gift one can personally give back to their being; the first is love.

I have known Adele for several years now. She has been a beautiful soul within our global innerdance community and a powerful voice in relation to bringing visibility and insight to the many processes we share across the planet. Our community focuses on healing, wholeness, consciousness awakening, and evolutionary transformation on multiple dimensional levels of experience and integration. What Adele is able to mirror for the world speaks not only to a personal story of patience, growth, and transformation but also to a globally building awareness that is made resonant through her ability to perceive the wholeness from within the parts, as she simultaneously integrates parts into the whole. The meta-narrative that connects a collective of stories together makes visible a becoming as we share dialogically in the spaces in between.

When I was young, I had memorized a specific scripture one summer for Vacation Bible School. This scripture continued to reverberate in my head for years to come as the very first sentence was the most meaningful for me and my journey, especially in my late teens and early 20's. The verse is from 1 Corinthians 13. Verse 4 states, "Love is patient, love is kind." Love IS patient. This became my affirmation, my vision, my heart. As I read Adele's words, I could truly feel her writings vibrating within me as she, too, refers to this way of love. How beautiful it is to intentionally hold space for love as patience. With patience, we might just find the windows that also open up to trust, kindness, and compassion – both for our loved ones and especially for ourselves.

The strength of character it takes to journey into one's life experiences with a knowing that everything happens for a reason and that it is perfectly meant to be, just as it is, does not come easily; our social, cultural, religious, political and familial structures hold strong systems of interpretation within the constructs of our minds, perspectives and world views. The more we are able to hold space for trust in the unknowns that live and breathe within us, even when we might think that we already know an answer, solution, or fix to what seems problematic, wrong, or bad, the more we expose ourselves to a greater consciousness that speaks of an empathic intuition that both transcends emotional boundaries and seeds intelligent wisdom. As a guiding principle, we will always find ourselves more whole when we gain insights and clarity through self-reflexive processes of continuity in relation to reciprocity, trust and love.

Before Pi Villaraza, the founder of innerdance, transitioned into a two-year silent hermitage in our ecovillage home in Palawan, Philippines, he passed most of his current roles and responsibilities, within a number of international networks, into my care. I now hold trainings for all dimensions of the innerdance energy school (ides), am a Vision Council member for the Global Ecovillage Network of Oceania and Asia (GENOA), the Integrative Director for the Self-Health Empowerment Movement (SHEM), the main organizer for Emergence Convergence events, a leading partner with One World Bearing Witness (OWBW), and a key advocate for Wholeness Systems based on the frameworks of the Eastern mandala. My main focus is bringing dialogic processes to communities across the globe committed to empowerment through that which is made visible when we speak the unspoken and give rise to that which emerges from the spaces in between. We are learning to remember as we remember ourselves; who we are, why we are here, and what exists within each one of us that transcends all separation – and together, we make visible the new meta-narrative of a planet through the evolutionary process of conscious transformation as we dream it into being.

— Serena Olsen
Puerto Princesa,
Philippines, 2017

Love with Passion and Perspective

The Hague Convention on the Civil Aspects of International Parental Child Abduction 1980:
Removing a child without permission from a country that has signed the treaty means that one parent can accuse the other of child abduction under this international treaty.

Habitual Residence:
When moving abroad with your children, if you end up separating from your partner, or if one of you wants to stay in the foreign country while the other wants to go home, you might not be allowed to return home WITH your children.

PART 1:
WHY THIS MATTERS?

CHAPTER 1:
UP CLOSE AND PERSONAL

YOU COUNT. YOU MAKE A DIFFERENCE.

Many lives are impacted by cross-border divorce and the Hague Convention. I believe that we meet such a delicate circumstance, because on some level, part of us had a need that is hidden from the basic human senses, to develop greater capacity to live our own lives and evolve our souls.

If you are reading this, chances are, you or someone you know, is experiencing divorce that is quagmired in the Hague Convention, even though the content of this book could be quite refreshing and largely relevant to anyone who picks it up.

The Hague Convention on Child Abduction is unlike other laws about children: Although it is fundamental to international child law, in the Hague Convention the child's welfare is not paramount. Instead the Hague Convention on Child Abduction regulates which country has the power (jurisdiction) to decide where the child should live, namely the country where the child was habitually resident. The Hague Convention then provides for a return to that country. The Convention is a treaty about where the jurisdiction of the courts of one country ends and that of the courts of the other country starts. It must therefore be seen in a line of international treaties that demarcate boundaries, similar to those about fishing rights etc. If a return is ordered, that does not mean that the court has found that it is best for the child to live in the country where it came from and the courts there may well give the parent permission to relocate later on.

Reference:
http://www.alternativefamilylaw.co.uk/international/hague-convention-child-abduction/

The way this is implemented differs considerably from country to country in every case, sometimes more holistically but typically in a clunky way. This book was first conceived during the review process of my first book, *Live Your Whole Capacity*, long before my second divorce. At the time, I was working with both my spiritual mentor and my spiritual guide. Together, we gathered there was more I could share in *Live Your Whole Capacity*, but for some reason, I either held back or the circumstances were not ripe for further revelation. More than a year later, a strong felt sense arrived, as if to tell me that this book is complete.

From feeling that sense, to putting it into form, became a journey in and of itself. For one, the sense of completion was ironically catalysed by my decision to file for divorce.

The experience of a divorce was challenging. Complicate it further with a young child in an international context, and the cross-border laws add layers upon layers of complexity to what is already a difficult emotional undertaking. Bottom line was that the desire to protect my child and my ex-husband created the most resistance.

So, I began to ask:
- How can my experience serve others?
- How can I catalyse change instead of fight for change?
- How can I bask in well-being while doing so?

The reasons for these questions are:

I knew that we cannot create the future we deserve if we keep replaying victim stories.

I knew that if we make any one part of a system the bad one, from a systemic perspective, there is a high chance that our children will pay the price.

I knew that if we act from a place of anger or helplessness, the purity of intent is tainted.

I knew that we all have fears that hold us back from a much-needed, and even desired, breakthrough in love and life, and that personally, if I did not step into it this time, I would likely be forced to at some later stage under much less favourable conditions.

Ultimately, I knew that what I was willing to share will be of use to other people.

Love and Relationship, as a subject, has always attracted me. Throughout my life in the past two decades, I have met and been in and out of relationship with a few men.

Love with Passion and Perspective

Stories aside, being twice divorced, conventional rule would suggest that I am at utter failure at love and relationships.

However, wisdom illuminates the polarities in life, and while the law can demarcate, there is no clear black and white, even when it comes to convention. Life vibrates in many colours, let alone shades, mostly culture and values-based, whether we like it or not. Being an utter failure did not matter to me when I did not think or feel like one.

There is no lesson "out there" that is custom made for you, from which you can learn in order to shortcut your way to evolve. While there may be parallels with others, you have to walk your own path and learn from your own unique experience. It is your self-insight that unfolds a generative journey ahead, that not only differs in trajectory from history, but breaks stubborn and elusive conditionality, and expands your life path in a multi-dimensional way.

Sharing or not sharing one's experience and journey is a deeply personal choice that is regulated by a whole host of factors, some of which are beyond personal, human, control. The basic human need for belonging makes it more likely than not that someone somewhere will share something that someone else will resonate with. Correspondingly, support groups and activists keep mushrooming out of every imaginable challenge.

At the end of the day, however, this question remains: "What is our ultimate desire?"

Approaching anything in life with the idea that we need to fix something, presumes that there is something wrong and that there is a "right" way. From a standpoint of fighting for change, much is lost and any victory is but a losing battle.

Why do I say this?

Because *such is* the nature of duality.

However, all is not lost. We do have the capacity to live and operate from a different state of being, with a different vibe, thereby totally transforming how life plays itself. We simply need to tune in to that part of us, which remembers the expansion it is capable of.

THE BUILD UP

The human story is one that many can easily resonate with and make sense of.

When I decided to end my second marriage, it happened like a switch that flicked, as if I was hit by an invisible force. This invisible force was a culmination of a long build-up of momentum gathered over the years of asking the Universe for my deepest longings and desires.

The human story is one that many could easily resonate with and make sense of. I had very valid reasons and enough justifications to gather a huge fanfare. This pent-up energy served to counter any forces of shame and guilt that stemmed from cultural taboos and social expectations, which had been imprinted in the psyche, enough to propel a big change. But the human story is a matrix, and the matrix is meant to be experienced in order to know that it is IT.

Over time, I accepted that every experience in life is there to be of value, to serve, and inform one about what it is he or she is called to do. Every situation presents an opportunity to practice following the inner guidance versus acting out from the smaller ego base. I discovered that the switch flick could only have happened in our party of two as a result of BOTH asking in equal measure, for their deepest desires in freedom, growth, and joy. Finally, I understood.

Yes, there are the human lessons that involve discovering the problems, dealing with the human emotions as they come up in relationships, and tactics to make progress. This situation is no different. And there is no denying that the human journey is equally important, with all the practical movements it calls for. I will share some insights gleaned from my own experience as well as those of others who have been on a similar boat. However, I wish to set the context and tone for this book on personal growth, because I believe that by doing this, we absorb the experiences in ways that best serve us going forward.

As mentioned earlier, this book came into vibrational form when my book *Live Your Whole Capacity* launched, in the same month I decided to resume my divorce proceedings after placing a two-month hold on the formal process. Energetically, I remember simultaneously feeling birth and death, and all the emotions associated. It was one of the richest emotional experiences in my life.

I felt like I was being purified beyond measure, and what I mean by that is the experience of being washed through, over and over again, by pure ocean waves. It was a melting pot of exhilaration, fear, trepidation, curiosity, awe, disappointment, anxiety, appreciation and gratitude, in one capsule that promised to be a panacea, but that ultimately accelerated the "illness" of what the capsule was intended to cure. I was shot towards a "healing tipping point" through what seems like a process of "natural death in form," on the path of evolution.

It became clear to me that I had peeled into a deeper layer of personal growth, whereby my healthy-enough ego and personal boundaries were being asked to expand even further. I realised that the greater the challenge that is being presented, the greater the difficulty being experienced, the greater the call is for transformation.

Another way to look at this is to see that I needed this great challenge in order to build up the reserves of energy required to evolve. Therefore, for as long as we experience ourselves as being victimised or a victim of circumstance, not only do we remain stuck in helplessness, not only can we not change, we will literally be asking for an even greater challenge to be presented so we can accumulate enough pent-up energy for transformation.

Indeed, there are many things 'out there' that can be 'righted.' There are many people who need and will benefit from improvements in law and order, as catalysed by other people's pains. But this is not the only reason for this project.

I am writing this book because I want to pave a way for us to create a different reality by changing our narratives and changing our experience, regardless of what is happening around us, and direct our intentionality with grace. I want like-minded people to come together to co-create a more loving and inclusive reality that we prefer to live in.

In the process of my divorce, I came to know so many strong, courageous, and inspiring people, devoted to their causes arising from complex international divorces and various forms of domestic violence, who shine light on the Truth to accelerate positive change. I came across men who decided to own their part of the equation, men who "came out" to admit that they had been abusive or are challenged by issues with sex, safety and security that then plays out abusively in their relationships as the uncomfortable feelings are projected onto their partners in desperation to alleviate pain. I learnt that I can only take greater responsibility for our shared earthly experience and the lives of future generations by first tending to my own needs and emotions, and then on enabling an environment that lives and breathes security and love.

I hold a vision for us to find the best attraction point as activists, and join up to call for change from a place of loving allowance instead of angry fighting. Anger has a place in transformational change. I already see a lot of well-placed anger, and if we keep doing that, the light will eventually flush out the darkness. We could experience more darkness, we could feel more anger, but it does not mean there is more darkness and more anger; it simply means we experience and feel more. It means that the light is flushing the darkness away, so we can all start living from a new dimension, today. Ascension, evolution, growth, whatever we call it, happens here, right now.

Mindless fighting keeps us in a blind fighting spirit that is both exhausting and lacking in wisdom. Not only that, the minute we operate with the idea of "fighting" for positive change, we thread the fine line of potentially doing great harm to ourselves and others by swinging between the extremes of Victim and Perpetrator like a pendulum.

Yes, there are actions that impact people in very painfully felt ways, and we may feel strongly about convincing others about our position, in order for things to change. But if we can accept for a moment that our reality is perceived, if we can suspend judgement and release fear, we open our hearts to experience what we are meant to experience in our lifetime here on Earth.

You may be deeply suffering from the constraints of your context and presenting issues. You may want to change the world so people are saved from the pains you had to experience. You may also be a changed person yourself, having come out of your sticky situation, stronger and more passionate, to take on tasks that previously seemed too enormous, and you now play an active role in effecting the change you want to see in the world.

The important thing we must remember is that the energy with which our activating work is carried out makes a difference. To 'put things right' in and of itself assumes a tone of superiority and righteousness. And if we link external change with a result that we then judge as successful or not, we reinforce the belief we need to change our external conditions before we can accept our job as done. This is a form of resistance and if we keep resisting, we will unfortunately miss the point.

The Law of Attraction talks about soothing away resistances in order to allow manifestation of desires. Buddhist texts explain that dropping resistances leads to inner freedom that is not contingent on the outer. Christian scripture describes turning the other cheek and surrendering. Jewish scripture emphasises freewill and the sacredness in relationships. Hindu texts highlights that each individual creates his or her own destiny by thoughts, words and deeds.

The dropping of resistance is not an act of condoning or giving up, but a resolve that brings relief to the system, and leads to inner freedom that is independent of the outer structures. It does not mean to stop taking action, but to be able to live as freely and as healthfully as we can, regardless of the external conditions. It means stepping into our own power. It means taking responsibility and changing the game by playing on a different level, instead of defending or blaming. It enables action to be taken with free agency, without being driven by unconscious motives. It opens the portal to living and loving unconditionally.

This may seem counterintuitive to those who argue that in order to change the world and bring harmony, we need to fight harder against our enemies. But who defines the enemies and who perceives the other as enemies?

Fighting for harmony is like screaming for peace. It perpetuates the exact energy that you resent and brings forth more of what you don't want. This is the swinging between the opposites of Victim and Perpetrator, and we simply end up fighting ourselves. When we dissolve the battlefield, we step into a realm where no one loses and everyone wins. The caveat is that the result may not look like how you imagine winning would look.

As Albert Einstein once said, "We cannot solve our problems with the same thinking we used when we created them." In the new dimension, the old ways of doing things will not work. While bulldozing and pushing through may make things happen, this comes at a price. In the new dimension, we learn to allow things to happen.

As we get to know our raging energy and inhibiting fear, we let it catalyse what it needs to, and then move on. We can stay out of the hold of rage and focus on creating our best life by living it on a daily basis. As we focus on what is right for us, we steer clear from the impossible task of controlling the conditions of our environment in order to feel better, and we join forces to co-create with the whole of who we are. As we use the current experience to bring us to greater wholeness every step of the way, we learn there is no end to the moving, for the greater the growth, the greater the capacity to feel, and the further the finish line will seem to be.

"HAGUE DIVORCE" LESSONS

In creating a desired future, it is important to be less fussed about what has already happened and to put more energy into creating what is desired. But it is hard to avoid human stories when often it seems like that's the only thing the entire earthly world is interested in and wants to know more about: what happened, what was it like, what was said, what was done, why are you doing or not doing something, what are you going to do about it now and why? It seems to be our way of coping – by making something newsworthy or comprehensible, on some level, we find amusement and satisfaction, whether we connect with the story loosely or indeed, deeply.

By its very nature, words are limiting. On top of that, we can only "understand" situations through our own frame of reference. To know what I now know, and to see that everything is borne of creation, makes the retelling of human stories somewhat meaningless. But without the human stories, that which needs to be shared has no container nor context to hold energy for any personal understanding that can ease application of any learning in real time.

This divorce brought to light so much more than my old self could have fathomed. It is neither better nor worse than I imagined, just different. What I can imagine today, having moved through the divorce, I can only do because of what I am becoming.

With inquiry, something... anything... will not be what it seems.

What became even clearer than ever from this experience is the role of emotions and how attending to it like you would tend to the signals a baby sends out... with open, kind and loving presence, brings forth the forces that shift energies. What emerges from the human is guiding light. It is this process that I wish to honour. Our emotional guidance system is the master controller of our lives' creations.

Many people have said to me that they are "in transition," and I smile, because we are in constant transition. The difference lies in the magnitude of the energy being gathered to bring to form what already exists vibrationally. Therefore, there is no beginning and no end to any transition, only a felt sensation that something big has gone, something new has come, and there is more that continues to unfold.

I intend to share some common lessons from the various scenarios I encountered in the course of my international divorce, as well as offer reflections that may seed your own sense-making and be of use to you regardless of your personal circumstance. I appreciate the challenge in this because we receive messages differently when we are on another part of the journey. However, with a little awareness, we plant a seed that holds potential for sprouting at exactly the right time.

The common themes I found in international divorces are:

1. The cases start off in the direction of being contested, even though they might not end up so.
2. There is a point of no return exacerbated by situational complexity, whether the divorce was planned or not.
3. There is a trend for the divorce to be about the rebalancing of power dynamics.
4. There are sophisticated threats, blame, and justification, particularly in the beginning stages.
5. There is violation of boundaries to the point that can be viewed as abuse and domestic violence.

Quite pertinently, I found that there was practically a competition of victimhood and blame, i.e. "You did this to me" versus, "No, you did this to me first" or, "You are crazy and totally responsible for this mess" versus, "It's all your fault, you asked for it and it is too late to mend now" or, "You are mean and manipulative" versus "No, you are the mean manipulative one," etc.

The divorce process in and of itself is fear-led and therefore it is no surprise that we find so many horrific, true accounts of divorce going pear-shaped, spread like wild-fire on the internet and social media. The legal process presumes the worst-case scenarios and creates a mindset that aims at covering all bases. It feeds on human insecurity and societal judgments inasmuch as it tries to protect social welfare, fairness and human interest. As such, the process has the potential to bring out extreme behaviours from the darkest recesses of a person, and many are shocked by what is said and done as the divorce kicks off, despite already being somewhat prepared for an avalanche.

The ability to hold light and tend to one's own needs, despite all that is going on, is the key to realising the positive potentiality for personal growth, which can then move one towards enabling the well-being of the entire family system.

This is the highest calling for those on the divorce path.

There are plenty of support groups out there offering emotional, legal and empowerment support. The most common tones are either empathy in the sadness so people feel understood and loved, or encouragement and allying in the fight against the other party for justice. There are a few in the helping circles who manage to direct the sailors in the winds of divorce away from victimhood and vindictive empowerment, towards the truth of what it means to step into personal power.

I learnt so much about the dynamics of violating relationships; relationships where there exists in one form or another narcissism, co-dependency, misogyny, bullying, domination, intimidation and covert incest, where verbal abuse, emotional abuse, sexual abuse, and downright psychological abuse could take place without a shred of physical abuse, thereby making such violating behaviours immensely difficult to evidence; i.e. the "new domestic violence."

Not only that, sophisticated forms of abuse, such as narcissistic gaslighting, can turn against the recipient the moment matters are brought to the counselling room and litigation. Trying to prove it makes matters worse as judicial manipulation goes on in great elegance, putting the 'victim' on the defensive. Energetically, this simply does not feel right.

Once I got my footing in the new norm, supported by some transformation tools, I realised that the changes were unfolding multi-dimensionally, across time and space, and beyond time and space. There can never be a fight for justice when to win means there is a loss, and when fundamentally we are all energetic manifestations, thereby what we are really fighting is ourselves, and we remain "trapped."

What I want to say to those who are in an international divorce situation is this:

> **You are called onto this journey because of your strong desire to evolve and to become that which you can only become from this experience. You have a tremendous capacity to love that which wants to come out and play. There is great love for you.**

If there is one message that I wish for you to receive from this book, it is that you are of most service to humanity when you are of service to yourself, and you are of most service to yourself when you use any negative emotions as an inner compass to guide you to align with who you really are. Because when you are aligned with who you are, you have love to give. As long as you are looking to another person or thing or situation to be what you want in order for you to feel complete or whole again, you will never arrive because you are looking for alignment, looking for love, in all the wrong places. You are stronger than you give yourself credit for.

We may want our conditions to change because we believe that when some things change, we will feel better, and we may well be right. However, if we depend on the change in conditions in order to feel better, we become victimised by powerlessness when things do not change in the way that we want or at the speed we want, because controlling the conditions of our environment in order to feel good is an impossible task.

The Hague Convention was established with a positive intent and its abuse is a reflection of the extent of human desperation when the survival mode kicks in.

I know, almost for a fact, that my situation would have unfolded differently if not for the Hague Convention. My ex-husband would have believed and acted differently and my daughter and I would have had different options and opportunities available to us if there was no Hague Convention.

Given the history of how our relocation came about and my reasons for turning into a trailing spouse so heavy-heartedly, had I known that I would never be able to return home with my baby, I would never have left without putting things in order such that I could return with no issues. Of course, without the Hague Convention and all the complexities it threw onto my path, I would not be the woman and mother I am today, but this truth does not negate the need for a change to the Convention.

With the existence of this Convention, the choice remains either to go with the flow, or resist. Either way, the ultimate destination or goal can be the same, but the experience, the journey and the unfolding situations would be different.

THE HISTORY

The purpose of the human story... the history... is to spark change and draw resonance to move towards greater clarity on future design.

I touch on the history for that reason. What seems like an overnight breakup was truly a culmination of deep-rooted, long-standing vibrational intention, the momentum of which could only be brought on by BOTH parties until tipping point. It takes two to tango, as they say; the what, why and how of everything that unfolded is a joint contribution.

About a year before I decided to file for divorce, I faced a situation whereby I had to let go of my struggle to keep the family together, by honouring my truth. I told my ex-husband that I did not want an open relationship. He asked for it the year before, and six months after he first mentioned it, I agreed. I wanted to be loved and I believed it was a loving act to do what I could to be supportive towards him. I rationalised away my uneasy feelings to a point where it was comfortable enough for me. I even got excited about that journey out of sheer curiosity and I thought it would bring us closer. I also believe it was a path I was meant to walk, because if not for that, I would not have grown in my capacity through what I experienced.

I thought I was aligning with my values to keep the family together. But as a wise saying goes, you cannot build over a flowing river; eventually the river breaks through. Six months later, I realised it was not for me (at least not yet, and not in the ill-informed situation I found myself to be in), but I feared what this would mean for us as a family. When I finally grew enough courage to deal with a complete meltdown of my marriage, I spoke my truth, and faced all ensuing consequences.

During that time, I asked and received the following guidance from my teacher, Pi:

You've been preparing for this inevitable part of the journey. You're at a point where there is no space to doubt that this, too, is an act of creation. Painful as it is, it is beautiful. A Soul chooses to experience love often in the most difficult of ways. In that, your Soul grows and finds its purpose.

Love seeks not weakness, but to make of us, independent. Love is not attachment but of pure perspective. When love loses its perspective, it is not love. It has in it, fear.

In your case, love splits in different directions. This is so because you are asked to split between loving your husband and your daughter, which is a very indirect powerful way that points back to you, loving yourself over them both. Loving them all the while but the you in them. Which is asked to be cleansed and detached.

Bringing this into perspective is to just love without people in the picture. The people are mere constructs for energy to pass through. They are all of them you. The monogamy-polygamy part of it are illusory constructs for your Soul to shift its awareness of its own capacity, its wisdom, power, and in this case independence.

Issues like safety, stability, morality and belongingness come about. The concerns of the human mother and earthly partner who often lands upon this Earth to experience the journey of loving so terribly much that she might rediscover herself after giving so much of what she feels inside. And is then asked to love herself and not place any part of her essential heart aside.

The guidance was profound and it continued to work in me for weeks and months. These words stuck with me the most:

Love seeks not weakness but to make of us, independent. Love is not attachment but of pure perspective. When love loses its perspective, it is not love. It has in it, fear.

As fate would have it, after three weeks of silence, I received an email which said, "I choose to stay in the marriage, but I know I can choose out if it stops serving me." There were no further conversations on this topic. Even though I knew that since I said I did not want an open relationship he could continue to explore his sexuality in ways he thinks is appropriate, we mutually avoided the topic and never talked about it anymore. The irony was that I felt as if there was a betrayal, even though technically there was none. Mapping this out through my systemic understanding with support from my colleague Anutosh, I realised later on why – trust had been broken in the family system, and we were both responsible for it, and responsible for not repairing it.

This incident hastened the decline of the relationship, even though on the surface we were both holding up. We both recognised the erosion of intimacy over the year, until finally, we could not hold us together through the biggest contention that had been spewing for five years. Our major differences in values, intimate lifestyle preferences and opinions, in particular my need for a shared vision and my feeling cornered to agree with and execute his plans, was the final straw that broke the camel's back, snapping me out of my trance, for the lack of a better word.

Two days after a fateful, intense conversation, as if by Divine intervention, I was at a performance called Finally She Spoke, directed by Sangeeta Nambiar. It was a collection of true stories of the struggles of women globally. One of the stories was about the imposition of the Hague Convention on an expatriate mother, effectively holding her 'hostage' in the host country after her divorce. My heart sank as I realised I may never be able to return home with my child.

The silver lining was that the Hague Convention forced me to look closely at my marriage. Without the Hague Convention, I might not have inquired into and discovered the deeper underlying causes of the breakdown of my marriage; I would have only been able to experience the stories. It also heightened my caretaking sense to ease my child into the transition.

I never realised that I held so much fear in the relationship and I kept hanging on in order to keep from facing the biggest fear of not being able to cope or handle his reaction. Given what I was holding on to, I realised that my love had long ago lost perspective. I kept leaning into fear, and surprisingly, one day I found myself saying, "I'm not going to allow my fear to stop me from choosing what I instinctively and intuitively feel I need to do. It did not stop me from trying to buffer fear, but eventually, fear did subside, even if it did not disappear altogether.

Most importantly, what emerged for me as I went into hibernation mode to gather energy for change, was that the last straw did not break the marriage; it was the catalyst that led me to the evolution of how my ex-husband and I are to relate going forward. I knew I had to be stronger than my fears and step up so my child could continue to be the child regardless of the pull for her to accelerate her growth, and despite the threat, the intimidation and hypocrisy that I feared would come.

Four days after the news broke formally, my ex-husband and I made an agreement; that I would pause divorce proceedings to attend the Hoffman process, which he attended, to help us shift the dynamics of our marriage. In exchange, he agreed that he would support our daughter's transition to school back home, so she could begin kindergarten at the age of four a half. I agreed to go, despite genuine concerns. The six-week wait to the process was rather agonizing.

From a learning perspective, I had a breath-taking week with a group of beautiful souls and a dedicated faculty, and together, we gave ourselves totally to the process. There were several magical moments for me, but what is relevant here is the insight I got about how over-thinking, self-doubt and validation-seeking persistently showed up in a vicious cycle during extremely challenging times, and how this showed up in my marriage. I realised that the divorce was particularly challenging for me because I did not like being labelled or thought of as the bad or wrong one for initiating the divorce. It triggered unhealthy shame and this hidden lack of self-worth brought on the vicious cycle of needing to explain and be understood; it led me to being victimised and placing myself in a position of having to defend myself.

I saw that my identification with being "the good girl" played up the pattern of being vulnerable and helplessly attractive to men who were wired to "rescue" and "take charge." I found it almost impossible up until that point to stand my ground with authority figures, and I had placed my ex-husband as an authority figure in my life.

I chose to see my act as "selfless" and "good," with the excuse of being spiritual and working on my ego. I played small and inadvertently allowed the other party to become the bully, growing in the sense of entitlement when in fact, he was capable of greater light. I was more comfortable feeling angry or sad and right or good, than bad, wrong, guilty, misunderstood or ashamed. I attracted people who had no qualms taking charge, and under different circumstances, that was a relief and I was familiar with that. But circumstances and people change. Consequently, the experience of reality shifts. It has to.

I saw more clearly than ever that I could never return to my marriage despite feeling deep love. This was not easy to explain, but in the end I found my energetic footing, and everything began to click into place. I did not have to be the right one or the good one. I recovered further from unhealthy childhood patterns and dissolved another layer of dependency that attracted and brought about unhealthy behaviours into my life.

Ultimately, I took responsibility for my own creation, as healthy empowerment began to blast away the deeper layers of legacy patterns of behaviour and conditioning. When I accepted that I had unconsciously co-created my entire experience, and therefore no one is to blame and no one is guilty, I let go of the narrative that kept me living in the shadows of my past. I began to allow more fresh and new thoughts, feelings, and experiences to come to my life, and I began to feel inner peace and joy, so much so I had to remind myself I deserved to feel that good even whilst going through divorce. I knew there was no more room for guilt, only a focus on taking responsibility, choosing positivity, and creating dreams.

The divorce process was terrible. I was warned about the language I used with my ex-husband; if I said "I love you" or was too caring, my divorce could get thrown out by the court. I was wary of sharing my raw feelings because it had come back to bite me before. The process was simply a platform to deal with marital split in the most efficient way possible. Despite positive intent, court-mandated counselling sessions did more harm than good, save for creating time and space for some natural healing to runs its course. Well-meaning counsellors may be working with limited background, time, scope, and cross-cultural experience. At the time of my divorce, I felt that there were perhaps more complicated cases with narcissistic gaslighting for example, than there were experts with experience.

From the moment I began to take steps towards divorce, I lived with anxiety and feared the worst. The more I did not want to fight or go to litigation, the more I seemed to attract situations that brought me down that very path. I basically kept creating exactly what I did not want. One fine day, I finally let go. I cared less. I thought to myself, *if I have to go into litigation, then I'll accept it and walk the path. If I have to pull out evidence and "defend" then*

I accept it and deal with it. The minute I made that shift, everything changed for the better. I was no longer fighting my own fear of losing control over how things could unfold, and detached from my desire to part amicably, even though it was still a wish. I allowed guidance such as this one from my friend Vera to arrive:

> *"If you have lawyers, it's best to deal with things through the formal channels. It would be great if you both could agree not to speak badly about each other to and in front of (your daughter). Stay strong and reciprocate by focusing on his positives as a dad. As your daughter grows older, she'll form her own view. Let her defend you. She'll know when Mummy isn't the person he says (overtly or otherwise) she is. Fighting fire with fire results in destruction. If you can bring compassion to inappropriate behaviour knowing it's coming from a place of hurt and not retaliate, it'll take the heat out of your exchanges. You don't need to justify anything to him nor react to his comments aimed at hurting you. That's when you step into your power. And keep reassuring (your daughter) that both Mummy and Daddy love her very much and that will never change. You will emerge more powerful and more aware of who you are and what your purpose is as you step into your freedom."*

It struck a chord. It was a stressful time and we were all subject to our own means of coping. But I kept remembering:

> **Fighting fire with fire results in destruction. If you can bring compassion to his inappropriate behaviour knowing it is coming from a place of hurt and not retaliate, it will take the heat out of your exchanges. You will emerge more powerful and more aware of who you are and what your purpose is as you step into your freedom.**

I was blessed with support and physical space to practice this. I think this guidance serves anyone walking through divorce.

It is with gratitude that I conclude The History. I had perhaps the top mediating Judge handling my case, and an intelligent ex-husband who shares my deep love for our daughter. The legal structure held space for the human expertise and life practicalities to play out, at least for my case, while the shared love moderated the process to help shape an outcome we could live with and make work.

When I consider my situation compared to other divorcing couples, I feel very blessed for all that I am surrounded with and I feel very loved. No doubt my story has its pain points but they seem to show where the glitters are, and integral to the artwork of a masterpiece whenever the silent one looks upon it with detachment, in absence of cynicism, judgment and doubt, and in pure vibrations of nature.

I am truly and eternally grateful to have experienced my ex-husband for all that he is and all that he is becoming.

Maybe it seems easier for me to do this than many others who have different, perhaps more challenging conditions. Ultimately, we need to see through the fog and pick up every piece of blessing along the way to anchor our movements, however ironic this may sound.

I have created amazing things with him and now I carry him as part of me as I continue on my life's creation. To me, a family can never really be 'broken up'. How a family looks from the outside can vary in so many ways, but a divorce, more often than not, grows it and enriches it, **providing** this is what we consciously choose moment by moment and deeply believe it to be so. We are better co-parents because I can direct my thoughts accordingly and fully embody my part of the equation regardless of his part. There are few who can believe that I love him dearly, that has never changed, no matter how many other negative feelings are co-mingled with that. And if I could do it all over again, I would still choose the same – to meet, marry, and start a family with him. I am taking responsibility for a path that I know aligns with our greater purpose and it meant initiating change in a way that I could never have practiced but one in which I could only activate with the best of intentions.

My ex-husband and I both experienced how the different energies can come out to play depending on the state of our being. This alone contains enough lessons and training, if you may, how not to suppress, repress, control, vent or act out each big piece of energy making its way through... but to watch as it comes and leaves our system... and this learning is a journey of living a vision that is constantly being refined every step of the way.

I have seen us both when we are at our best human selves. I have seen us operate and make decisions from our highest potentiality. I know the lives we are capable of living on a day to day basis. On this account, I know that whenever I choose to focus on how our daughter is thriving and believe that she is growing in her own way regardless of conditions, I enable that for her. Whenever I choose to bring light and evolve options towards thriving rather than surviving, I multiply the positive impact I have on everything I touch. And whenever my ex-husband chooses the same, we will find resonance. This is the resonance that brings about systemic healing, well-being, and pure love. This is living in flow with nature that brings about Whole Systems Capacity. If my ex-husband was to hold tightly to the belief that the divorce was messing her up, he would be right, because children do their best to live up to their parents' expectations. It is so important to choose thoughts that create the story we deserve.

It was so common for people around me to ask how our daughter is coping with all the changes, feeling rather sorry for her, when in fact, no one truly knows which path would turn out "better." I prefer to believe that children are super adaptable, resilient and wise beyond years, and our role as parents is to support them in connecting with who they are. If children are forced to take sides or understand and/or validate either one or both parents, they are forced to split off from who they are, and never truly feel settled as they continue to seek approval from forces they encounter in life, forces that trigger the same reaction that their parents had triggered in them.

THE FUTURE

In *Live Your Whole Capacity*, I talked about the source power for change. While anger and victimhood may seed a change, it can never supply the necessary momentum to balance and sustain transformation. The only true powerhouse for change is Love. Our human mission is to drop resistances and allow inner wisdom to lead the way. Then our whole capacity grows with change.

But how to do that in the midst of challenging situations?

When there is a lot of negativity going on, talking about it keeps one in that energetic space, somewhat suspended in time, despite physical time moving ahead. Negative inertia compounds and one remains "stuck." You may encounter different faces and different places, but the same sort of pattern keeps repeating. Catch yourself early enough in your spinning of the same story and you clear the fog, enough to see alternatives. It is not an easy undertaking because so many things keep you in the fog, continuing to spew mist that keeps the fog going.

It is normal to react when something is coming at you, but if you keep spewing negativity, it will be very hard to do something else, and you must get out of that defensive place to focus on better feeling things so you can soothe yourself into improving what comes your way. Believe that there must be value in this situation still being worked out, and remind yourself of who you are. As long as you are looking to another person or situation to change in order to make you whole, you will never arrive, because that which you seek is within. Even when that which you desire is out there, you can ease yourself into feeling whole, unconditionally.

Many who find themselves in victimising situations are not used to taking back their power, but the good news is that therein lies huge potential to make a change, to reclaim what seemed lost, with graceful kindness once conscious actions are imbued with light in a clean, clear way. You may be pained by the difference between what is happening with what you want but this gap brings clarity as to who you are, and this clarity could well be what you want more than life itself. It could well be what serves yourself and your entire family line and wider community. And it is a journey.

It is easy to feel loving when people are being lovable. It is easy to feel good when the conditions are exactly as you like them to be. Unconditional loving, unconditional living, is less easy. Being able to stay in the vibration of well-being, in alignment with source or what some call Truth or Light or Higher Self or even God, regardless of the conditions, is true freedom... that is the epitome of what Love is.

Well-being is when one is in vibrational alignment with source even when things are not what one wants. Well-being is when you can start acknowledging people and situations as they are when forgiveness seems like a leap, but it does not mean you need to continue to engage and let it affect you. One thing's for sure: conditional love will never get you to where you want to be. I found Abraham Hicks' guidance held me in a space that allows unconditional loving by affirming:

> *I love you so much, I don't care what you think. I so care about being in vibrational alignment with who I am because if I am in vibrational alignment with who I am then I have love to give, but if I am catering to what you want rather than my own guidance, then I have nothing to give. I love you so much, I must tune to the source within me but I cannot tune to the source within me and tune to what you want at the same time. I see you as you really are, not as who you are being in this moment. My love for you is unconditional. I am no longer going to hold you responsible for how I feel. I am in charge of how I feel. I am so good at unconditional love that I don't need you to know how to do it. You are not the boss of me, I am. I have the ability to align with source regardless of what surrounds me. I get unconditional love.*

I love you so much, I don't care what you think. I see you as you really are, not as who you are being in this moment. My love for you is unconditional. I am no longer going to hold you responsible for how I feel.

These words fed me like "raw whole food medicine."

Loving with passion and perspective is an act of unconditional love. It requires you to love deeply as a human being without losing perspective or at least recognise when perspective is lost. Loving with passion and perspective means no longer playing the victim of circumstances. It means uncovering and releasing beliefs that are in the way of receiving desires. It means letting go of attachments to a particular, painful version of the story. It means loving in a balanced way, applying wisdom to compassion, and practising resilience while trusting in the goodness that is unfolding. It means attracting love by fully enjoying the present moment.

Yes, we want laws to improve, people to be well, behaviours to change, but our work, our growth, is to be able to find satisfaction regardless of whether or not these desires come true. If we activate anger and frustration in working as an activist or advocate, instead of focusing on what we have immediate control over and catalyse change from there, all we do is create more of what we do not want and perpetuate strong negative emotions. The dawning of a new era tells me that we cannot do things in the same way as we have done in the past. We have to quit our fixation on fixing.

A powerful way to shift our trajectory is through the process of expansion, and one part of the journey is experiencing expanded consciousness using modalities that we like and that we have access to. This includes still or moving meditation, breath or energy work, inner-dance or sacred dance, using plant-based medicine, including raw foods and essential oils, dialogic processes, art-play, listening to healing music, choosing company that support our new choices, and consciously fine-tuning the body to pick up more subtle frequencies and energies. We can practice living a different trance, in a more creative, generative, dreamy, yet awake mode. In this tone of living and working, we allow our actions to arise as guided by spiritual forces and return to wellness.

If we tried to resolve issues only in a physical way, we would be bound by human limitations resulting from past conditioning, which already had strong specific momentum to create reality in a particular direction. We may experience a change of scene and people. Fundamentally, however, nothing has truly changed. If we are unable to soothe ourselves to a breakthrough, we will never be able to truly effect a change because we are not there to receive it.

In the issue of upgrading the Hague Convention, if we drop for a moment all the BUTs and IF ONLYs that short-circuits innovative processes, and feel into the change that is desired, we are already closing the gap before the law even budges an inch. By deepening the understanding of WHY, reducing the resistance from short-circuitry, and allowing the HOW to emerge instead of directly tackling the WHAT that needs changing, we immediately bring about the trajectory for change and multiply the speed of change. This discussion continues in Part 3.

****

I will be sharing NORA's story. NORA is a fictitious character created from a composite of true stories from all over the globe – USA, Japan, Germany, Russia, UK, Zimbabwe, Singapore, and so on. I have attempted to condense and present layers upon layers of the inner workings of a human being who ultimately deeply desires personal and spiritual growth.

Using all my training and experience as a human and organisation development professional, a mother/ex-wife, a facilitator of truth, a wholeness practitioner, and a change catalyst, to deep-dive and map out a fluid framework, it is my desire that readers can take what they read, internalise it and make it their own.

It is narrated in first person so that the story comes to life through resonance for shifts to occur, which one can only get through one-to-one conversations, to deeply illustrate Part 1: Why It Matters?

After NORA's story, I asked a dear colleague Hillary Munyoro, to share his findings and reflections. Part 2: Unpacking the Hague Convention, aims to shine light on the darkness, with the intent of collecting generative energy to bring us closer to a future we collectively desire.

Coming from Zimbabwe, a country that is not party to the Hague Convention, his work showcases the suffering brought about because of the limitations of the Hague Convention. The intent of the Convention was positive but while it may seem like the right thing to do, when misused and enforced, the Convention can make one parent a criminal and the children abandoned in favour of the parents or the law; the adult employing an ego-centric thought process rightfully believes in the law to a tee, whereas children are unlikely to understand it in the same way. In cases where there is domestic violence (of the sophisticated kind or otherwise) and no parental alienation, further judicial manipulation literally condones one party's 'killing off' of the other.

Smear campaigns aimed at fighting to win our children back compromises the well-being of the child. Complicated domestic violence is difficult to evidence and victims often fear that no one would believe them, until it is too late, and the system has a high tolerance built into it. What constitutes abduction, and the general lack of awareness about the existence and implication of this Convention on the global lives we lead merely scratches the surface of the deeper considerations to the issues arising from the Hague Convention, and each local circumstance needs to be addressed. If so many people are suffering from this law, if so many people are being led by fear, then we have really lost perspective here... our love has lost perspective as propelled by law.

It is way beyond the scope of this book to discuss the Convention in detail, especially considering the complexities introduced at national level. BUT, there are things we can still do, as NORA's Hague story mentions. Mandating all families relocating due to work changes to be fully briefed about the Hague Convention and given a Pre-Emigration Contract to discuss and review within two years is one such example. GlobalARRK champions this and has been putting forward proposals to amend the Hague Convention. This practical element is discussed in Part 3.

Suffice to say, we need a new narrative. Just as we collectively co-created what we do not want, we continue to have even greater clarity about what we DO want, COLLECTIVELY. So let us sing a new song, speak and act with that clarity, from that clear, unconditional, open and loving space, from that moment of pure potentiality, no matter how fleeting.

CHAPTER 2:
NORA'S HAGUE STORY

No law can govern family love.

No court order is above the order of family love.

Love heals.

From the early days of when we landed on the foreign land I noticed the way he treated me changed. I brushed it aside, rationalising that he was simply stressed about the new job, new country, new baby coming, new role as the sole breadwinner... as evidenced by arrythmia. Inside, I wished we would be financially free as soon as possible. I focused my attention on my pregnancy, regulated my own stress levels, and looked forward to motherhood. Nevertheless, his behaviours continued to disturb me and we sought professional help, which kept our relationship ticking along.

He never hit me. He encouraged me to pursue my passion. He said he loved me. So, I never considered my marriage to be abusive until one day, Providence moved. A sophisticated argument left me feeling battered on the inside, totally betrayed, bullied, trapped, angry, and deeply disappointed. All I could think about was hatching an escape I never realised the amount of fear I avoided facing, and the false sense of love and security I retained by confusing myself simply to keep my blinkers on. But overnight, I saw him as a different person. Something about my perspective shifted big time and I could no longer not see what I had refused to see before.

Some days later, I learnt about this thing called the Hague Convention. It was one of the most devastating days of my life. I felt simultaneously betrayed by my ex-husband and the system. I had left my home and the life I loved to trail him halfway across the globe, gave birth to our baby there, became financially dependent, sold our house back home, took up residency in the foreign land so he had employment flexibility, even buying a property there for investment… all the while, unknowingly setting myself up to be controlled whilst digging my own grave from a Hague Convention perspective, until it came time for me to digest my decision to divorce.

I figured I had to get legal advice. The Universe must have had a grand plan because I got the wrong advice. A reputed expat divorce law firm told me that if I wanted to file for divorce and return home, the steps I needed to take was to get consent to go home even if it was for a short holiday, and instruct the firm from there to begin proceedings. I asked her about overstaying and the Hague Convention. Her answer was that he would have to put things in motion to bring me back, and he may not do it. She was asking me to play with fire, and I did not know.

A month later, I finally got consent to go for a holiday,

only to learn when I landed that I had been misguided. A kind local lawyer firmly advised me to return to the place I fled and handle the matter from there. Nevertheless, the two weeks away gave me the space I needed to settle what I now know to be Level 1 emotions and sort through some practicalities. My ex-husband's business was not going well, and I had offered on several occasions in the past to return home, get a job, and support our transition. He disapproved of that. So when he smelled that I was trying to get work back home, he went into a rage. He accused me of manipulating our child to ally against him, issued a warning and threatened: "Be careful. You could well go back but without a marriage and without (our child)."

I sought counsel, and after one session, I was given reading homework. My jaw dropped as I realised how many check boxes for abuse my situation ticked.

References:
https://www.justice.gov/ovw/domestic-violence
https://www.womensaid.org.uk/information-support/what-is-domestic-abuse/
http://www.refuge.org.uk/get-help-now/help-for-women/recognising-abuse/

Despite the positives that I valued in my marriage, I was shocked by how unhealthy it had been; how far I was from the wellness I was capable of and so deserved. However, I could not bring myself to put those on the divorce papers. And I surprise myself with my first reaction being:

"Who would believe me?"

My ex was a high-profile expert in the helping profession

with a reputation and gravitas to behold. I was privy to his character while others know mostly his personality. Only a handful of our mutual friends and colleagues would have had a chance to witness how he spoke to me and his demanding and domineering ways. I practically regretted going for couples counselling and sharing my feelings with him about us all these years since he had direct interest to steer me in a particular way whilst being blind to his own agenda.

If I crossed him with abuse, he would stop at nothing to turn the table. He is effortlessly smart, manipulative and charming. Many women who met him for coffee or lunch would have at some point sat in front of him and cried. A decade ago, I was one of them. He has strong judgments and opinions about Asians as an example, and in this regard, he would say that I was stunted in my growth, over-sensitive and cannot take jokes, a coward only capable of passive-aggressive behaviours and that I behave like a paralysed terrified child.

He crossed ethical and personal boundaries, for example, by seducing a neighbour's wife without her husband's consent (despite him being his friend), texting her from our bed at night to set up a date and when I showed annoyance he said I was controlling, impossible to live with and incapable of handling jealousy.

In one scenario, he arrogantly defended his right to seduce her without consent, flatly dismissing my opinion about his professional ethics and boundaries to which his response was that I did not know what I was talking about. And I believed him! Until I got professional help.

By this time, two parallel processes were well underway:
1. Why and how did my marriage reach this crossroad?
2. What do I do now?

I researched and learnt more about how I behaved as a result of unconscious dependency and relationship addiction adaptations, and how that fed his coping mechanisms that included narcissistic, misogynistic and fantasy addiction adaptations. The more difficult he became, the more he drew me in, as my belief in my capacity to heal him through love increased with my spiritual practice. I faultily believed I was the special chosen one for this irrefutably tough assignment, and that if I loved him enough, he would heal and be happy. Finally, I could see how they presented themselves in my unique situation. I began to understand the dance of darkness we had been engaging in, all twisted in a deadlock.

Although I was still digesting disappointment, anger, guilt, grief and fear, once I understood, I felt the shift towards something new that was inevitably healthier, happier and more abundant. Even though I felt violated and abused at the time, I no longer felt compelled to behave in the helpless righteous ways of a victim fighting for justice. I was drawn to self-care and self-responsibility and I allowed all the intuitive guidance within and without to lead and pave the way.

The road was still bumpy of course, but I figured that no one who bullies and abuses power will knowingly admit to acting inappropriately and agree to being dumped without putting up obstacles, to put it mildly. I may not have consciously been aware of being in an abusive situation, but on some level, my being knew. Otherwise, the situation would have unravelled differently, and I would have chosen differently.

As the mother and primary care person for a young child, my self-responsibility IS the core of taking responsibility for the immediate well-being of my child. I learnt to walk the fine line of balance between what's best and what's right, choosing intuitive conviction and responsiveness, instead of validation-seeking and scenario-planning whenever I could.

My over-riding concern was how he would react to the fact that I was serious about the divorce, how the next weeks and months would unfold in a country that was not my home, where could I go when our lease was up, how our child who was fast approaching schooling age but nowhere near starting kindergarten, would experience the covert bullying and tension once all these come to play?

I had no other choice but to depend on the foreign jurisdiction. Had I delayed filing and discussed divorce with my ex-husband, I ran the risk of him filing ahead of myself in his birth country where we got married; a jurisdiction with an infamous history in terms of family law, especially after his threat.

Reference:
http://www.reuters.com/article/us-divorce-citizenship-dual-idUSBRE89N10V20121024
https://en.wikipedia.org/wiki/Divorce_Italian_Style
http://www.imdb.com/title/tt0055913/
https://www.uniassignment.com/essay-samples/history/divorced-italian-style-and-seduced-and-abandoned-history-essay.php

I was fortunate to have met a lawyer who formally trained in handling cross-border divorces that could trigger the Hague Convention. She was also the only one who met me without asking for any payment upfront. I engaged her immediately and filed the papers.

With so many moving parts, all I could do was be guided by my own intuition and instinct. I needed them both in equal measure. It was a particular challenging period whenever he was in my field, and especially at the beginning of the court process. I remember the first time I was in court, I could not believe how anger and fear would lead my ex-husband to lie, put words in my mouth, essentially fabricating "evidence" by virtue of smearing through "facts" and sound like one of those Hague Convention statements you read off the internet.

He demanded that I returned with our child instead of taking temporary shelter at my parents a stone's throw away albeit across the border and intimidated me with the Convention. He threatened to lodge a criminal report against me for abduction if I did not do so, and until our child was returned to him, he would not commence any mediation with me. He also refused to come to see our child in order not to set a precedence and so he could maintain the story that I had wrongfully abducted his child. All the while, Skype time, video and audio messaging continued as before. I found the hypocrisy unreal and kept feeling anger rising up from my belly each time he flipped from being super horrible to me and being super nice to our child in an instant. During court counselling, he threatened again to be prepared to fight in court and to forget about ever leaving the country with his child.

He argued that because I had planned the process of the divorce without his knowledge, I had deceived him, completely over-turning his agreement to consent to our return home. But if I had not considered the well-being of our child and I simply left without our child, not only would it have been too irresponsible for me, I could be charged with child neglect and abandonment and lose custody completely. There was no way I would return to a hostile and abusive environment towards me without clarity on agreements and boundaries. If I could, I would. The alternative of talking to him was simply going to go down the route it had always gone; gaslighting.

There are limits to couples counselling and I have come to believe that if not careful, it leads to more damage than good, particularly when the couple divorces and the process enters litigation. Even when done 'properly,' the relationship counsellors' job is to keep the relationship, sometimes at all cost. Technically, they cannot counsel the couple out of the couple because that typically is not what they are contracted to serve.

Being in an intimate relationship with a professional helper battling narcissistic adaptations meant living with the following triple-edged sword:

- What is shared gets coloured by cynicism, and hypersensitivity to imposition and judgement.
- What is brought to the discussion almost always turns into my deep psychological fault and responsibility to fix.
- What is done by way of action gets measured against

an unknown standard or expectation that ends up being criticised with a gloss of praise.

I developed a three-pronged response:
- State my truth
- Choose silence
- Accept limitations

This coping mechanism helped me to strengthen my personal boundary, nurture the human guide that accompanies the spirit's human experience. The energy I had previously put into dissolving my egoic self was due to my misjudgement that the ego is bad, and I thought I was practicing the elimination of the ego in order to evolve spiritually. The insight was that the ego exists to act in a service-based relationship with spirit, to bring harmony and balance to actions in response to intellect and emotions, through this vehicle of the human body.

GASLIGHTING

The mandatory couples counselling sessions brought back the visceral response and reaction of gaslighting when we were living under the same roof.

Gaslighting is a form of abuse that instils anxiety and confusion until the victim finds it hard to trust their memory, perception or judgment, similar to techniques employed in psychological warfare by intelligence operatives. No wonder I felt tortured every time I entered into an intense conversation with him. He would say, "Just bloody answer the fucking question!" Through coaching, I learnt how to meet him… that I could choose not to answer his questions in his way, and to think for myself in my own way.

I identified my ex's behaviour with the five common actions associated with gaslighting:

1. Withholding: Your partner pretends not to understand you or flat out refuses to listen to you. He or she might say things like, "I don't want to hear this again."

2. Countering: Your partner questions your memory, even if you're sure you know what happened. They say, "You're wrong, you never remember things correctly," or "You're imagining things, that never happened."

3. Blocking/Diverting: Your partner changes the subject to silence you or questions how you're feeling, saying things like, "Is that another crazy idea you got from your (friend/family member)?"

4. Trivializing: Your partner makes your needs or feelings seem unimportant, constantly telling you that you're too sensitive, or that, "You're going to get angry over a little thing like that?"

5. Forgetting/Denying: Your partner pretends to have forgotten what really happened, or flat out denies promises he or she made to you. He/she will say things like, "I don't know what you're talking about," or "You're just making things up."

If you identify with these 10 signs, you're most likely being gaslighted:

1. You are constantly second-guessing yourself.

Love with Passion and Perspective

2. You start to question if you are too sensitive.
3. You often feel confused and have a hard time making simple decisions.
4. You find yourself constantly apologizing.
5. You can't understand why you're so unhappy.
6. You often make excuses for your partner's behaviour.
7. You feel like you can't do anything right.
8. You often feel like you aren't good enough for others.
9. You have the sense that you used to be a more confident, relaxed and happy person.
10. You withhold information from friends and family so you don't have to explain things.

Source: https://www.davidwolfe.com/10-signs-victim-gaslighting/

It is a form of abuse by individuals displaying narcissistic adaptations, like my ex who:

1. Has an exaggerated sense of self-importance.
2. Is preoccupied with fantasies about success, power, brilliance, beauty or the perfect mate.
3. Believes that he can only be understood by or associate with equally special people.
4. Requires constant admiration.
5. Expects special favours and unquestioning compliance with expectations.
6. Has an inability or unwillingness to recognize the needs and feelings of others.
7. Is envious of others and believes others envy you.

8. Behaves in an arrogant or haughty manner.

Reference: http://www.mayoclinic.org/diseases-conditions/narcissistic-personality-disorder/basics/symptoms/con-20025568

I found these seven points about narcissistic behaviour particularly succinct:
1. A narcissist has conditional self-worth.
2. A narcissist constantly needs more validation.
3. A narcissist is motivated by intense fear.
4. A narcissist uses anger to avoid feeling deeper emotions.
5. A narcissist operates from an all-or-nothing perfectionist viewpoint.
6. A narcissist has his or her own set of rules.
7. A narcissist's behaviour has little to do with you.

Reference: https://www.mindbodygreen.com/0-27567/7-underlying-truths-a-psychologist-wants-you-to-know-about-narcissistic-behavior.html

Putting these together, narcissistic gaslighting behaviours showed up like this for me:
1. When I no longer toed the line, and refused to simply follow his desires and do as he wanted to expected, I was told I was crazy, disrespectful, "unilateral," "chicken" or that I did not know what I was talking about.
2. When I did not shower him with praises, blanket him with hugs and kisses or did not show enough excitement and agreement with his projects and plans, he got upset and I was told I was cold, frigid, disconnected and unsupportive.

Love with Passion and Perspective

3. When I shared parenting experience, research and opinions, concerns and considerations, he got territorial and I was told I was imposing, obsessive, suffocating, too controlling or too lax, too enmeshing, and need to either be "put back in place," or simply dismissed.

4. When I brought my unhappiness relating to our relationship and home front, he got annoyed and I had my feelings and intuition questioned, invalidated or twisted to what suited his priorities and processes, so much so that I began to feel selfishly guided by him to his advantage.

5. When I became more "bothersome" I was told that if I was not happy "just f*g do something about it"... as if bringing it into conversation, including mentioning separation several times, was not enough evidence of my doing something about it.

6. When I asked him to relieve me of baby duties when my child was six months old for half a Saturday so I could finish my project, he got annoyed at my "poor time management," said that I chose to do chores when he is around, and questioned how "wisely" I spent my day.

7. When he had performance anxiety or could not have satisfying sex with me, I was told I was boring, uninitiated, not adventurous/curious/giving enough... but when I took the feedback and made improvements, I was told "is that it?" or I was pressuring, too passive, or gave up too soon.

8. When I filed for divorce, I was told I was crazy, we had a beautiful marriage and that he will not allow me

to destroy 'his family,' that it was a bad decision for 'his child' and that I was throwing the baby out of the bathwater.

Then I looked up narcissistic counsellors, therapists and practitioners on the internet.

> *The narcissist, **because of their lack of trust, sets their own agenda**, and this is likely to be on a "You Don't Need To Know" basis, where **they withhold information from the therapist** about the own core wounds of abandonment and rejection.*
>
> *If you know what to look for, it is not hard to spot the narcissistic therapist. You will soon find out that they are fixated on power and money; you can gleam this by the way they **cannot resist speaking about their personal lives in an egotistical way**. Their pursuit of monetary gain is so great that it often leads them to **keep their clients engaged in the therapeutic process longer than necessary**. Their need for admiration is so great that **if their client should dare to disagree with any point they make, they are bound to be punished** (verbally, or by emotionally withdrawing from them), they have a real need to be comfortably superior.*
>
> Reference:
> http://www.psychforums.com/narcissistic-personality/topic78062-10.html, http://thenarcissistinyourlife.com/narcissistic-psychologists-psychiatrists-psychotherapists-prey-on-desperate-individuals/

I was then led to Dr Judy Rosenberg's work. The penny dropped on the first YouTube video I watched, which was about the people-pleaser and the narcissist, and how they are a "match made in Heaven and Hell."

Reference: http://psychologicalhealingcenter.com

And finally, I found Richard Gannon's 20 Signs You are with a Covert Narcissist super spot-on.

Reference: https://youtu.be/-WVLZXLyO-M

The more help and support I allowed into my field, the more I allowed my inner voice, information gathered and insights arising, to power up practical movements. I practiced recalibrating my sense of what is the truth:

HE SAID	WHAT I HEARD	THE ANTIDOTE	WHAT I SAY NOW
You are throwing the baby and the bathwater. I am dumb-founded.	I am guilty for throwing the baby and the bathwater.	Guilt trips no longer work for me.	I'm taking responsibility for my well-being and that of my child.
You're unhappy. Go and do something about it.	It's my fault. He is not hearing me. I am abandoned.	It's not my fault. I am heard differently. I am not abandoned.	I am looking into my dissatisfaction and I will know what I need to do in the right time.
You're stuck in old stories.	I'm the one with the problem. I'm not good enough.	I am not the only one with a problem. I am enough.	I'm not stuck but I am taking responsibility of my old stories.
You have a low threshold for conflict.	I'm not strong enough.	I'm sensitive. I do not need dramas.	I am fine even when there is conflict.
You are such a coward. Bloody grow some balls.	I'm not brave enough. I am afraid of him and what is to come.	I feel fear and I lean into it.	I have courage and I can be brave. Everything will be okay.

HE SAID	WHAT I HEARD	THE ANTIDOTE	WHAT I SAY NOW
You keep breaking my balls.	I'm too aggressive and demanding.	I'm assertive in my own way.	I am truthful.
You are suffocating and intrusive.	I need to back off and stop asking questions.	I just want to be close and loving.	It is normal to desire love and intimacy.
You give up too easily.	I'm not resilient.	I am keeping up.	I am strong and I am resilient.
You do it your way, I do it my way.	I'm excluded or I need to be individualistic in this relationship.	I'm radically inclusive and I'm open to collaboration.	We do it our way and sometimes we are in sync, sometimes not.
You keep staying in the victim mode.	I cannot talk about my suffering.	I want to take responsibility.	I am empowered by self-responsibility.
You have zero personal conviction. You have a feeble sense of self.	I don't know who I am, what I want or if I am doing the right thing.	I feel some doubt but it is okay.	I trust in truth and I allow my intuition to act as my inner guide.
You were talking crap, fixated on home base, so the phone fell.	I am tongue tied, stupid, and wrong. He is being mean.	I value my emotions and speak truthfully despite my fear.	I trust in my truth and intuition. I'm strong, confident, and enough.
You are such a hippie it's not even funny (eye-rolling)	I am not accepted for who I am.	I am not seeking validation from him	I am enough.
Your vision is so boring.	Oh no, how are we going to grow as a family?	I can hold onto my vision because it is healthier for me to do so.	A simple family life just does not appeal to him, I am OK.
We don't need a shared vision for our marriage, family and future.	He is selfish and does not care about what I want.	I want one even though he thinks we do not need one.	It is ok to want to develop a shared vision and I deserve it.

As that began to clear up, another layer unravelled: what was I most worried about with regards to our child?

Could I co-parent with him? Do I honestly believe he will comply to the points that I raised? I began to talk about the points I raised as I developed the parenting plan with a psychotherapist, a psychotherapist-in-training, an intimacy consultant, a sexologist, and a registered nurse, and when alarm bells rang from ALL parties, I knew my instincts held true. I was then pushed to do my own desktop research, read many books, and wrote to the National Society for the Prevention of Cruelty to Children (NSPCC) for guidance.

I was advised to seek protection immediately. I was also asked to consider the drivers for my ex to practice in the helping profession with the area of interest that he did, and to ask myself if there was a chance that his chosen vocation was an unconscious behavioural cover up for sorely un-integrated aspects of his whole? How could I continue to walk on eggshells, believe in false hope and live with blind faith?

Reference:
How to Co-Parent With a Narcissist
https://youtu.be/kZqX1-TTD0Q

I was so torn, because nothing terribly bad has happened to our child that could be evidenced sufficiently, and with the Hague Convention, as well as research on family systems and shame, I was super cautious about what to do. Running for protection would only anger him, as knowing him, he would have thought I simply cooked up an excuse. Having my child questioned could have made my child feel wrong or ashamed!

What dawned on me was that if I made him the perpetrator, the family system dynamics could result in my child living him from the place of a child's loyalty, and I would be manifesting the very block I was trying to enable flow and heal.

No matter what, he is the father. I believe it is important that our child grows up healthy and can honour him, the him in our child; the aspect of our child which is like him that is well-adapted.

Therefore, when it came to discussing access terms, I listed many provisos that the court counsellor was supposed to help us address. She never fulfilled her duty in helping us have that conversation. My guess is that she was afraid of the consequences, especially given that she would not have much time with us. My ex tried to brush it aside as a difference in culture and values, but being more informed, I was confident in maintaining my point. However, I could not explicitly put everything into a court order because it would trigger his rebellion and flag the authorities with abuse, without necessarily protecting my child.

The legal advice I received was that if I wanted protection, I needed to file a personal protection order, but if I did so, he would not be allowed near my child. I was told not to complicate matters further since mediation was seeing progress. I had to allow room for trust, and to some extent, accept that our child came to Earth with a unique birth vision and life path to walk. I can only guide, I cannot control. I had to surrender to all the pain that was going through my whole being, to really understand and embody what it means to look at my life experience and feel into what I am called to do because of the life I had been living.

I felt that my courage began changing things, and I kept praying that my ex-husband's love for our child would continue to change his behaviours now that light was being shone on it. I also summoned strong belief in my child's capacity to nourish the self and live the best life... to trust that my belief would help enable that in our child, and that our honest and clean relationship would continue to serve us in truth.

After two months of court case conferences, mandatory counselling, and mediation, my ex-husband agreed to my returning home with our child. The big movement was when he told me he is trusting me, that it was hard for him. While I was relieved that our biggest contention to date was effectively over, I was disappointed that he did not want to return together, despite telling the judge during mediation that the intention was always to return, it was simply an issue of timing and my fixation about returning home. He stated clearly to me in reply to my question about his plans and timing for return, that he had no intention to do so.

Nevertheless, he met me on a heart level. However brief, I was grateful for that glimpse of light. In the past, when such glimpses showed up in my marriage, it filled me with delusional hope and kept me handcuffed in the golden cage. Now that I am clearer about what we, as a couple dynamic, were up against, and the patterns of behaviour, I am far more realistic and less judgmental. He still blames me, but thanks to his blaming and my experience of gaslighting,

I kept learning how to relate to him in new ways while saying goodbye to the old ways no matter how hard it was. I pray that I continue to be mindful and retain hope and appreciation against all odds.

Footnotes on narcissistic behaviours:
https://www.pinterest.pt/pin/195343702568369319

An excellent summary video on Trauma Bonding:
https://blog.melanietoniaevans.com/how-to-recognise-the-5-types-of-trauma-bonding/

Having settled my divorce by foregoing maintenance and picking up repatriation and legal costs, I have a few wishes as a dependant trailing expat wife:

- Compulsory insurance: The person or company who applied for the Employment Pass must also take up an insurance policy for the spouse and children with a minimum premium of $100,000 or minimum of 50 percent of the annual salary, which would cover legal fees in case of divorce and financial support before the court establishes spousal maintenance and/or relocation.
- Escrow account: The Employment Pass applicant must open an escrow account where 10-20 percent of the monthly salary be deposited for the same purpose as above. This would ideally be part of the immigration process in granting an Employment Pass. This account should only be available to the spouse and children in the event of a divorce.
- Update the law: The financially dependent spouse should stand equal in court with the breadwinner

footing the legal bill. That emotional, psychological, sexual and divorce abuse be treated in equal standing as violence where there is physical evidence. That fleeing "captivity" and further bullying, intimidation and manipulation, with the children, is not "abduction," especially if all the while, contact is present.

• Upgrade company briefing: All family members relocating with the parent who has the international job should receive full briefing about the Hague Convention and its implications, as well as discuss and sign a pre-emigration contract that will be reviewed within an agreed timeframe.

I cannot turn back the clock, but having experienced what I have, in a good way, I would not want to, for the contrasts in my experience all bring me towards closer alignment with my Truth.

The signs were there from the moment we dated. One simple example was my 'mild discomfort' at totally being controlled ("taken care of") during our first holiday whereby he planned everything and ordered for me at meals without asking what I liked or did not like. And when in his eyes, I failed to show enough appreciation, he could not hide his utter disappointment.

Some weeks later, I found notes at his place from a couple of years before, on a previously planned holiday with one of his ex-girlfriends, that bore a similar pattern as mine. In hindsight, I saw so many other episodes where I ignored my instincts and intuition, and rationalised them away, making up excuses for him, all in the name of romantic love.

His disrespect of rules, ethics and diversity, and his demanding expectations at work and as a customer receiving service, is energetically similar to that of a slave master. He would not hesitate to get the cleaners to 'pay back' any accidental damage, and if implemented, it would mean they each would have to work overtime weekly for three months just to repay a vacuum cleaner, for example. He seduced women with partners including four known to me who hinted to me but I did not heed them. He broke local law and rules and a mother's requests on safety, that he deemed did not apply to him, like not dismounting himself and the child from the bicycle in the underpass, using the stroller on the escalators while the child was in it, and shaking the stroller when the 3-week-old child was crying instead of allowing me to pick the child up, and when I insisted with tears in my eyes, he said "you are so f***ing annoying."

I never saw his controlling nature until the divorce because my behaviour was wired to be pre-emptive of conflict. I was completely transparent with him while he guarded his 'privacy' and 'personal space.' For one whom many had commented was overly trusting and generous in giving benefit of doubt, I lost my trust in him completely. So much so that when he said post-divorce that he will always be there for me and our child, it triggered disbelief as a result of the many occasions when he used my vulnerabilities against me.

He prided himself when I looked good to others. He would lie in court and express tremendous anger towards, me, yet in the next breath, tells others he respects my decision, that I am a good woman with enormous capabilites and heart, but due to my fears and insecurities, I kept our child away from him and her habitual residence. He would say to me in the presence of our child, "Just you wait. One day she will know what you have done."

In my situation, he shape-shifted in times of conflict and heavy conversations. He expertly sniffs out what I say and sculpts arguments over me in the same way that in happier days was seductive and charming. I do not believe that the majority of people get married preparing to divorce, and hardly anyone goes overseas as a family preparing to disagree as to where home base ought to be. And it is unthinkable to think that at one point I wish I had recorded all our conversations, the demeaning, threatening, intimidating, manipulative, verbal and non-verbal language he used, sometimes with great skill to disguise anger and vindictiveness. Couples counseling may have ended his habit of name-calling, but it never healed the place with which such behaviours stemmed from.

My ex and I agreed very early on that the host country was not a place we would settle and school our child. Despite agreeing on our return within a timeframe, he tried to change it several more times during the reconciliation period. Instead of supporting our transition, he told our child when our lease was up that "we are moving to our **own** place" (referring to the rental flat we owned that he suggested we move into for practical reasons) and she continues to refer to his flat as the "real home" while the previous place we rented was not. He would teach her through play that "it is good for us to be alone" (i.e. without me) and "this is our home forever" (at the playground of his flat). When I asked about childcare while I would be away, his response was "what I do with (our child) when you are gone, is none of your business." With these actions taking place during our reconciliation period, I could not see how they served her instead of him.

Through support groups, I found that it was not uncommon for dominating, misogynistic and narcissistic reactionaries to proclaim themselves to be good partners and parents in over-compensation even if no one judged them to be bad. These folks expect you to laugh when you are being put down. My ex would say "why don't you just shut up?" or blatantly put his hand up to my face. Over time, I got better at doing the grey rock and one day, after we already divorced, he said that again. This time my child turned to me in that instant to say, "I love you, Mama." My confidence in my chosen path to divorce and live separately was further strengthened by the clarity of my child's intuition and balance. Her love for the both of us and her courage to speak her truth in that moment of cold conflict was testament of at least one unhealthy pattern broken.

Shadows may fleetingly haunt, but I remind myself constantly that today is a new day. Every day is a new day. I love him deeply, but how I relate to him today is different from before, and even this is evolving. I am suffering a lot less than I used to, and I would like to think this is a result of expansion. If I cling to our past stories and all the things he did and take zero responsibility for being party to it, I would be holding onto blocks and giving up my true power to change my world. How we are today is made up of how we arrived into this biographical life, which is transpersonal. How we were grown in our formative years and what we choose on a moment by moment basis continue to shape this. Would I have been the way I did if I did not carry unhelpful shame and guilt? Would my ex-husband have behaved the way he did if not for the burden of unhelpful shame and guilt? Who is to blame? While there are people who *could be made* guilty as such, ultimately, who can we actually blame? No one.

People who push boundaries are calling out greater and deeper efforts to know boundaries more clearly, to know expansion and limiting beliefs, to know unhelpful patterns of behaviour, such as self-loathing, self-doubt, self-blame... to know unhelpful shame and guilt that has been worn for years... and to finally decide if it is time to shed them off and let them go. What happened is for me to know and for us to grow as a collective.

Reference:
https://blog.melanietoniaevans.com/what-is-narcissistic-abuse-really-telling-us/

PART 2:
UNPACKING THE HAGUE CONVENTION

CHAPTER 3:
A GLOBAL VILLAGE

"The world is now a global village."

Or is it...?

Certainly not from the viewpoint of a parent scorned, for lack of a better descriptive term for the way a parent feels when their child is taken away to or stuck in a foreign country in the name of the Hague Convention.

Picture this...

Two adults meet and love runs its course, blessing them with the gift of children. Later on, life happens to them, as it does to all humankind, and they decide to go their separate ways. Then the all too common beast rears its ugly head before them... *Who takes the children, and who sees them when...?*

Normally, this is part of a familiar part of the separation process whose family-law-dictated settlement is widely predictable, even when relations have taken a nosedive. But it's not that straightforward if we introduce an international twist to it.

One parent is either a foreigner wanting to return home or simply wants to relocate to another country *with the children*. That's when they realize they are trapped in a web, created by legal entanglements, which have nothing to do with the love they have for their kids or how they are going to express it as freely as they ought to.

For the uninitiated, this is a rough introduction to that part of the Hague Convention which directly affects international parent-child relationships. Together with those who have already crash landed within its perimeter and those who are fast approaching its borders; here is a message of solidarity, hope and a possible way out of such legal commotion.

The World Doesn't Seem Like the Global Village Anymore, Does It?

Technology has made it easy to keep in touch with loved ones when they are away from us. There is certainly no shortage of communication channels, which literally bring sweethearts a tad short of a physical embrace. And we all bless the souls that toil in order to bring us such convenience, and make such effort to lessen the burden imposed by lonesomeness when those dear to us are beyond arms' reach.

Well, that is just technology and it will always be as virtual as it has ever been; lacking the ability to transmit the warmth of a kiss, the comfort of a hug or the assurance of a pat on the back. For parents living in a foreign country, those planning to relocate abroad, and especially those stuck between home and their children, technology simply has not scratched the surface to bring down geographical borders around their love affairs.

While the world continues to preach about how everything has gone virtual, it is evident that authorities have made frantic efforts to keep certain aspects of life away from such efforts. But the sweet reality of love is that, just like technology, it knows no geography. It lingers in the air, and it always descends on its intended beneficiary, wherever they are. When love calls, who can ignore its compelling effect?

Yet the Hague Convention attempts to stop love in its tracks, albeit with devastating consequences. Sadly, the worst consequences fall upon the children who pitifully form the two ends of the rope which their parents use for their ugly tug of war charades. The same parents are not spared by this emotional battering. One parent is forced to become a parallel law unto themselves in order to answer the call of love for child. The other gets torn by the double-edged sword and is left to nurse both the wounds of divorce and the anguish of having their children taken away.

The pain endured by such parents is way beyond comprehension and only experience has found a fitting description for it. The idea of the world being one big village simply loses its essence, because geographical borders suddenly become real walls keeping them away from their deepest love.

WHERE THERE IS PAIN, THERE IS A WAY

Love is kind. Love endures. Love hurts when it is trapped within the heart, withheld from the one for whom it is intended. Whoever has love entrapped within them is propelled to act impulsively; and everyone will witness the uncontrollable eruption of love. Love is unapologetic and it knows no limits.

This is particularly true about parent-child love. While romantic love has been known to motivate people into all sorts of unthinkable actions, it is arguable that it stands no chance against parent-child love. What the Hague Convention has notoriously labelled 'child abduction' is largely, though not always entirely the manifestation of such eruption of love.

Moms and dads facing the possibility of being permanently separated from their kids are usually caught between expressing their love freely and maintaining their good citizenship. That's a tough choice to make, especially given the known fact that love can never be bottled up and stashed somewhere out of reach. Whatever and whoever fights with love, unfortunately fights a losing battle. The laws of love do not permit wastage of this precious emotion; love will be given freely (whatever the circumstances) or no peace will ever prevail.

To those outside the situations brought about by the application of the Hague Convention, child abduction is simply a crime committed by a desperate, uncivilized parent. But is that really all there is to it? Is it enough to ignore all the natural laws of love, which no mortal being is immune to, and trivialize the manifestation of love as mere criminal acts committed to fulfil some dark, selfish desire?

Surely, as global citizens who are subject to the same natural laws of living, love being at the core of it all, shall we knowingly entrap ourselves in legal technicalities which attempt to rid the world of the comfort of love? Why endure such pain if solutions lie right inside us, waiting to allure the world as they are unleashed?

THIS IS A MESSAGE OF HOPE

While important people in high places of authority probably never intended harm, the clauses included in the Hague Convention evidently declare war on family love. The evidence of how ravaging the Convention has been (and continues to be), lies everywhere for all to see.

There are multitudes of parents who have either suffered silently or have been branded outlaws by the dictates of the Hague Convention. At various points, the life courses of thousands of children took unnecessary detours while Mom and Dad took turns to shuttle them across borders. We will not even start to talk about the ravaging effects of divorce itself. The result shows up in a wide range of behavioural problems in both the parents and children involved. All these are mere symptoms of intense heartaches resulting from love withheld from its recipients.

But love is patient. Though painful, it can lie within our hearts for ages without losing its lustre. Where there is love, an abundance of hope thrives, keeping all hopes of finally delivering the wonderful gift of love alive. It is a gentle reminder to those at the verge of giving up that the world is about to collectively review it's take on matters concerning family relationships.

The Hague Convention is definitely due for a makeover,

which aligns it to make good the sad realities on the ground. That long-awaited makeover must happen now, so that the aggrieved souls around the world may finally step out of desperation and begin the process of healing. These changes will not be wished into place. The pain, which every afflicted parent and child feels, must motivate them to make their voices heard; to agitate, in their own unique way, for this change to happen.

These experiences are shared here with a view of exchanging possible solutions to various situations. But most of all, it is an attempt to bring awareness to those who are still uninformed about this piece of international law, its effects, and why they must call for its review. Throughout the pages of this book you'll find real life evidence of the devastation that the current laws are causing, and what could possibly be done to address the anomalies. May your faith in love receive a boost, so that hope is ignited within you and within your children, no matter how damned your situation seems in light of the current Hague Convention. Yes, there is hope in love, which we all have an abundance of!

CHAPTER 4:
WHY THE HAGUE CONVENTION FACES IMMINENT REVIEW?

Consider Sarah, a married mother of two living somewhere in the UK. She, her husband and two children are from Zimbabwe. They moved to the UK just after her daughter's first birthday. Her son is now eight and her daughter, six years old. Though, as a young girl Sarah had always dreamt of moving to Britain, she now wishes she had not relocated under the current circumstances.

But let us look at her story from the beginning.

Five years ago, when her husband Eddie called from work to announce news of his promotion, everything in her life seemed to have taken a turn for the better. Eddie had not been the best husband, really. He had been physically and emotionally abusive. And he had blamed it on financial pressure and interference in their marriage from relatives.

News about the promotion brought Sarah new hope for both her troubled marriage and her husband's attitude towards her and the kids. And her fantasy was confirmed that very evening when Eddie returned from work. He had not been that nice since before their son was born. Before the night was out, she discovered why he was in such a happy mood. His promotion had come with a condition that he had to relocate to the UK. In her mind, this literally meant that all their problems were going to be over quickly. No more extended family to interfere in their business, and no money problems, ever again.

Though Eddie had asked his boss for a day to 'discuss' the move with his family (like a responsible family man was supposed to do), the reality was, there seemed absolutely nothing to consider. Eddie and Sarah both needed a one-way ticket to the first world, where they could finally live their dreams. So, they grabbed the opportunity in a heartbeat and bid farewell to their Zimbabwean troubles.

A few weeks after moving to Britain, the first signs of the return of the old Eddie's bad temper showed up. He realized that although he was now earning far much more than he did back home, the general cost of living was way more than he had anticipated. The realities of living in a fast-paced economy were starting to catch up with him and he became increasingly irritable. He had promised Sarah he would pay for her tuition once they settled in Britain, so she could further her career as an Accountant. But now he had decided against that, and he started insulting her for being a lazy mom who only wanted to live off him. Sarah tried to look for work, but she soon realized her meagre qualifications were no good outside her home country.

Barely four months after relocating to the UK, she decided she needed to escape this abusive prison and return home with her kids to start afresh in a familiar environment. She could not make any decisions about anything, including her own life. She had no job, no money and no way to improve her situation unless Eddie changed his mind about taking better care of her and the kids. She knew a few people from back home, but none of them were willing to make a financial commitment to rescue her. Besides, most of them worked several jobs and hardly had time to understand her plight. Along the way, she approached Eddie and asked him to send them back home so she and the kids could live with her parents and ease his financial pressure in Britain.

To Eddie, this was a sign he had failed to make it in the UK and it was a huge dent to his ego. So, he said he would think about it, to brush her off. And that went on for months until Sarah took matters into her own hands and borrowed money for airfares. When she told Eddie she was going to leave with the kids at the end of the month, he simply told her she could not go.

Sarah did not understand what he meant. She dismissed him as an angry guy who did not think she could find the money for the airfares home. She knew he would struggle looking after the children since he was never home, so she was sure he was just venting his frustration. By now, almost nine months had passed since they had moved to the UK. And life there was not as glamorous as she had imagined. She wanted to return to where she could fend for herself and her two young children.

Then the weirdest thing happened at the airport. Just before Sarah and her two children boarded their plane out of England, she and her kids were taken by two policemen and stopped from boarding because 'Sarah was attempting to take off with two children.' She frantically tried to explain that she was the mother of the kids. But the policemen explained to her about how a piece of international law called the Hague Convention prevented her from taking her children out of the country without her husband's consent. She suddenly remembered what Eddie had said, this time fully understanding what he meant. To her, this was infuriating and confusing. He clearly didn't care for her and the kids anymore, so why was he stopping them from pursuing an alternative path to life?

Unfortunately for Sarah, she had to return to Eddie's house in Britain and endure the mistreatment. She had nowhere else to go where her children would at least live a decent life. Sticking with Eddie was her only option. At least until she figured out how to get around this weird law, she thought. As time passed, she started to piece together the complications of the Hague Convention, which had barred her from leaving her cold relationship and had somehow redefined her children's habitual residence to Britain, a country they hardly knew.

Sarah and her two children still live in Britain with Eddie, in a loveless and somewhat abusive relationship. She has visited her home country only once, by herself, to try showing Eddie that he would struggle if she left him with the kids. But he did not crack. Missing her children and worrying about their safety from their own father's irresponsible behaviour sent her right back to England where she is still in search of a more permanent solution to her troubled life, and awaiting the outcome of the never-ending legal proceedings.

Sarah is one of many parents whose family has either been torn apart or is in the process of being torn apart on the premise of the Hague Convention. And there are several abusive parents like Eddie who have decided to hide behind the flaws of the Convention. They simply use technicalities to further their selfish agendas.

LOVELESS HOMES ARE NO HOMES AT ALL

First off, the Hague Convention tries to redefine what a home should be to a family. When children stay in a Convention country for a few short months, the law automatically assumes they have taken on a new habitual residence. It immediately stops recognizing where the family has its roots, or where the family has lived previously. In addition, the Convention simply focuses on the children's habitual residence with total disregard to the parents' sole parental duty to directly influence the future of their children.

But as children grow up, they naturally develop a sense of recognition as to where home is. To them, home is a place where they feel safe in the care of adults (or an adult) who will do anything for their well-being. Home is where children are loved unconditionally, cared for endlessly, and made to feel happy.

Ideally, home is where Mom and/or Dad are. The true image of where home is, is a lot more than simply a place, building or country. It is a whole environment in which the best memories are surrounded by the most amazing feelings of love, comfort and total safety. Home is a place we all retreat to when the rest of the world crowds us out of comfort. Hence the good old saying, 'you can only build a house but not a home.'

This brief description of the true home is only the beginning of where the Hague Convention crosses natural family love concepts. By imposing a "habitual residence" on children merely on the basis of having stayed in a particular place for a specific period, the Convention literally destroys the forming of homes. One cannot simply declare or pronounce a home into existence. It unequivocally demands an investment in both time and effort, nurturing the love that's required to create memorable moments, which ultimately create the home environment.

Though the Hague Convention has made a declaration which seeks to use legal means to redefine what a child should call home, it potentially creates serious problems in a child's upbringing. One problem with this declaration is that it takes most parents by surprise. Whether it is out of ignorance of this international law or due to other circumstances, it is a trap for most parents.

The problems faced by people who move abroad are numerous; one of which is simply that things do not work out as planned. It is not unusual that emigrants decide to return to their home country when they face challenges in a foreign country. It is unlikely that parents facing this socio-economic predicament plan on leaving their children alone in a foreign country. That's unthinkable, to say the least.

The big problem with all this dismantling of the home

concept is that it causes long term behavioural issues in children. It is well known that children who grow up in loveless environments always wind up getting into all sorts of trouble. When the Hague Convention declares a certain country as the new residence for children; and their parent[s] have failed to make things work in that country, who then is there to make a home for the kids? Is this not a legal way of potentially damning the futures of innocent children?

Parents who have their children's best interests at heart have been calling for the relaxation of this part of the law for a long time, so it recognizes that relocation may not always be permanent. A cooling off period has been called for, in which parents are allowed to acclimatize to the country's social and economic environment. If they decide that things are not working out before the cooling period elapses, parents should be able to leave the country with their children without having to fight unnecessarily long legal battles. Of course, the decision of who leaves or stays with the children should be motivated by the parents' ability to provide a real home for the children.

DOMESTIC VIOLENCE

Besides the imposition of country of residence, it is increasingly evident that the Hague Convention has become a convenient tool for domestic abusers to take advantage of. Unfortunately, many domestic violence victims have been forced to remain with their abusers, courtesy of the Hague Convention.

Take Sarah, for example. The Convention has, for the past five years, barred her from removing her children from an abusive environment, simply because she cannot provide an acceptable alternative as long as she cannot return to her home country. This, and several other variants of the same predicament, has become a common modus operandi for habitual abusers, who thrive on the Convention's technicalities to entrap their victims.

It is estimated that at least 70 percent of all domestic violence victims are women. This means that men are generally the predominant perpetrators of this form of abuse. And interestingly, such abuse spans across many things besides physical abuse. Things like emotional abuse and refusal or withholding of financial resources are among the common issues surrounding women suffering abuse while living abroad. Being in a foreign country on their husband's visa, such women usually go without a job or any other form of income outside of their husbands'. When called to prove whether they can take care of the children, the case is obviously tipped heavily in the husband's favour. And unfortunately, this technical advantage gives a certain dark power to an already abusive husband over his exposed wife and children.

Another interesting statistic estimates that at least 67 percent of parents who resort to child abduction are women. As anyone would imagine, the stark correlation between these two statistics, coupled with the technical legalities imposing the habitual residence of children, evidence points to a huge problem, which the Hague Convention is silently fanning.

When the abuser is also the provider of life's basic requirements for day to day living, they wield immense power over their victims. The natural survival instinct kicks in, in different ways. Some people decide to endure the abuse for the sake of their children, especially when the abuse is not specifically directed towards the children. This is a sacrifice that most parents, particularly mothers, in such situations are known to make. Their maternal instincts seem to suggest that they should somehow be available to their children, even if all they can do is love them and teach them how to love abundantly.

However, in extreme cases in which harm is directed towards the children, the maternal instinct will likely stimulate a flight response, in order for the victim of abuse to keep the children safe from the aggressor. But getting away from an aggressor who's protected by the laws birthed by the Hague Convention literally dashes all hopes for the freedom to love and be loved.

Living in a violent or entrapping environment has never been known to nurture any kind of love. Instead, it breeds hatred, discontent and discomfort, all of which are repelled by love of the purest kind. Protection is one of the strongest natural parental instincts. It is not only evident in human beings; even wild animals display their need to protect their young at all costs, sometimes even to their own detriment. Anything that threatens safety or diminishes the ability of a parent to protect, automatically becomes an adversary.

It is this same instinct which stimulates parents to leave hostile environments and take their young ones out of harm's way. Unfortunately, for those parents who live abroad, this ability is threatened by the nearly impossible conditions set by the Hague Convention. The Convention rules create the perfect environment for an abuser to freely torture their victim. It creates dependency upon the abuser by the abused, whether temporarily or permanently.

Rather than try to dwell on the technical and legal aspects of parent-child abductions, which essentially criminalizes it, the Convention fails to look at the root cause, which is love. No loving parent would simply do nothing and resign to fate when their family is faced with any form of danger. When left with few or no options to protect their own, legalities may seem secondary to the safety of their loved ones, especially children who look up to them for protection.

It is therefore essential that the Hague Convention creates viable choices for parents living abroad but want to return home with their children. It is clearly not fair for such parents to be forced into giving up custody of their children owing to a legal technicality which lands them in a disadvantaged position. It is particularly unfair when statistics such as domestic violence, which correlate to so-called parental abductions, are completely unrecognized by the same international law, which purports to stand for the children's best interests.

DISREGARD OF CHILD'S BEST INTERESTS

This brings us to yet another shortfall of the Convention. The widely accepted family laws require that a mother has to be with her children up to a certain age. This has nothing to do with whether or not she can afford to do that on her own or not. Many countries have synchronized their legal systems to this nature-based rule. Though it is ideal for both parents to bring up children together, separations and divorce are a reality of the world today, and have been since time immemorial.

Separation and divorce do not always mean or suggest any loss of love, especially for the children. Therefore, when they occur, both partners usually agree on doing what is best for their children, so that they continue to express their love for them freely, especially when one parent is no longer living with them. As such, many parents are normally familiar with the outcomes of custody battles and even have certain expectations regarding children of a certain age. Precedence in many legal jurisdictions has it that child support and visitation rights is a significant part of the expected outcome.

There is a reason why this is usually so. Young children have a certain bond with their mothers and rely on her for most things. Whilst dad may play a different important role in the child's upbringing, there is a natural dependence that a child has on their mother in order to develop normally. Even before the moment of birth, a child depends on its mother for food. By the time of birth, her warmth, acceptance and love is already proven to a child. And so that natural instinct to love back the one who has proven to care as much automatically kicks in towards the mother. This bond never breaks, even if the child has a fallout with his/ her mother later in life.

Yet the Hague Convention simply ignores these issues and goes ahead to take very young kids away from their mothers, just because the child's "habitual residence" has been redefined. It is common to find children who were left with their fathers, grow up with an absentee dad who was always working.

Parenting is a job deserved by those who can make sacrifices for the best interests of their children, especially when the children are still young. It has nothing to do with the amount of resources one has. A good parent simply needs to have enough love to keep the children feeling safe and wanted. When love is not expressed freely, then a guardian ceases to be a parent, and the place of dwelling is no longer home for the children.

Parenting cannot be delegated to childminders and nannies. They are simply helpers along the way who cannot be held accountable for a child being deprived of love and care. Excellence in the job of bringing up children cannot be obscured by whatever number of gifts we may hope to divert children's attention to love, or lack thereof. Young children are simply laser-focused on receiving love, and reciprocating freely.

And so, it is in every child's best interest that they grow up with the parent who is most prepared to sacrifice everything else to achieve such a loving environment. Unfortunately, the Hague Convention does not always rule in the child's best interests; it stands rigidly on its pronouncement of a new habitual residence with whichever parent is prepared to stay in it.

PARENTAL ALIENATION

But perhaps the most damaging consequence of the situations created by the Hague Convention is parental alienation. Like I explained earlier, desperate parents may take desperate measures to be with their children. The worst thing that one parent could ever do is to turn the kids against the other parent, just so they can seem like they care more for the children. Parental alienation is one of the most desperate moves pulled by divorcing parents, especially in Convention cases.

The widely publicised story of Laura Garrett and Tomasso Vincenti immediately comes to mind. Following the events as they unfolded, it was clear that the parents, at some point, neglected the children's feelings to pursue their own agendas. Laura contributed in the breakdown of her family "because she missed her Australian home and family," and decided to run away with their four daughters.

Along the way, she and her family launched a smear campaign against her husband, Tomasso, as she later admitted in a televised interview. Tomasso responded by violently retrieving the children from Australia, with the help of the Australian police, based on the dictates of the Hague Convention. It was a regrettable sight to watch the girls being grabbed by grown men as they clearly resisted being taken away from their mother. Yet, it was not until 2015 that the girls also admitted they had been coached by their mother and grandmother to make their father look bad.

When parents fight, children suffer psychologically. They go through a period of confusion as they try to understand whether or not they are causing these fissures between the two people they love the most. It gets worse when children are forced into a position where they have to choose who to love and who not to love.

Feelings of love cannot simply be turned into the mildest form of dislike. Love is too strong an emotion to fade away just like that, especially in an innocent child. And this is exactly what parental alienation does to children, however convincing the smear campaign might be.

In the end, the truth always comes out, just like it did for the Vincenti girls when they uncovered their mother's lies about their father. Yet, it is not enough to get satisfaction from the eventual surfacing of the truth, as by then the damage has already been done. A lot of love would have been denied and withheld over time. And many beautiful memories that would have been created over that time would have forever been buried with mere fantasies that never came to life. That is the worst form of denial of love that a parent can commit and also force their children to conspire against someone they love dearly.

****

It is pure naivety to pretend there are no serious problems in dealing with divorces involving people from different countries, especially where children are concerned. These problems do exist, particularly matters around custody of children. Mainly, it is because if children are taken to a different country, the parent who is left behind is usually deprived of the same convenient access to children, which they would normally have if children stayed locally.

Admittedly, these are the sort of issues which the Hague Convention seeks to address. However, the manner in which it handles the same issues leaves it wide open to both abuse and unfair practices. It makes it easy for scheming parents to lure their partner and family to a country where they can better control them using the threat of losing access to the children.

We have seen how abusive Eddie used Sarah's lack of financial independence to trap her in an unhappy marriage and an unfriendly environment, all for the sake of her being with the children. These are real situations in which the Hague Convention is being used as a weapon against love, rather than an international tool to preserve family love and relationships.

These problems have serious consequences on the general well-being of many broken family members. There is widespread grumbling over how this piece of international law is causing more despondency than harmony between family members following a separation. Enough partners have resorted to illegal means of taking their children out of the country as a way of escaping the horror of losing their children forever. All that, because the Hague Convention does not consider the intricacies of both the emotional and psychological effects of the affected parties in the aftermath of the process. Essentially, it dwells on technical legalities when, in fact, it is dealing with matters of emotional and psychological consequence.

Men and women who have been deprived of their

parental rights or trapped in unfriendly environment for the sake of their children are silently uniting their voices to call for a review of the Convention's approach. As the number of voices multiply, the apparent inadequacy of the law becomes even clearer. Responsible authorities can no longer afford to ignore the pain being endured by affected families. And sooner rather than later, they will realize that the current state of the Convention renders it more and more obsolete in a world seeking to become one big global village.

CHAPTER 5:
HOW THE HAGUE CONVENTION CAN BE USED TO PROMOTE LOVE

As the world grows into a global village, love rises to its throne as the only acceptable, all-inclusive universal language. Whatever promotes love surely wields the unbelievable power needed to instil harmony among the multitudes of cultures populating the world. Can a product of love resist entrapment of the one emotion to which it owes its existence? Would all products of love not seek that which amplifies the source of their strength, the very root upon which their spirit thrives?

For ages and generations, mankind has recognized disintegration of family units as the one problem threatening the universal nature of love. The family is the cradle of love where it is nurtured and exchanged among parents, children and siblings before it overflows to peripheral relationships. Through the family unit, procreation brings forth new beings to carry the heartfelt message of love and blissful living, blending with the many other shades of love to create hope for peace and harmony throughout the land.

Thus, when the cradle of love starts to disintegrate, it is essential that the world does everything necessary to preserve as much love as possible. As far as this is concerned, the Hague Convention has immense potential to propel the spread of love, particularly when cracks start to form within the family unit.

However, before it can live out its potential, there is a dire need to rid the Convention of its obvious grey areas, which unscrupulous partners are repeatedly abusing. These are the numerous problems discussed in the first chapter, which we know to be loopholes used to disadvantage the other partner.

Deeper than being mere technical loopholes, these grey areas threaten the flow of love between parent and child, and between feuding partners. When it levels the playing field, so to speak, the Convention will create a fair environment in which divorcing parents can negotiate and agree on the easiest landing for all parties involved, especially the children. Parents will not gain any unfair advantage, or seek to dwell on loveless technicalities, which are only good for alienating themselves from their children and each other.

Separations can be more civil, even though they will be no less painful. However, a civil separation leaves room for healing and reconciliation of emotions at another level, which is way above the romantic relationship of parents or the scorn felt by the parent who misses being with their children. The difference is that each party has a chance to develop understanding of what the other felt and why things happened the way they did, bringing about a sense of closure to such difficult life experiences.

Aayesha, a Muslim woman living in Australia acted out in real life; a near perfect response to a similar (bad) situation, all for the sake of preserving relationships. She and her Algerian husband were living in Australia with their three daughters when one day the husband simply picked up the children and disappeared with them. Aayesha was left to face the horror of imagining where and how her children were living, until she tracked them back to Algeria, a non-Convention country.

Despite knowing they were in Algeria, she struggled between locating them in the country and the non-cooperating legal system, in an effort to retrieve her children. Although she had the ability to fight her case through various means, she decided not to keep fighting and risk exposing her children to the ensuing trauma involved with such legal battles. She reasoned that they were already suffering serious trauma from being with a father who was determined to constantly be on the run from the law. Tough as it was, she decided to give her children a little peace and stability by abandoning her pursuit of them. Instead, she decided to try and resolve issues with her husband without involving the children.

Aayesha's children, who are now old enough to speak and decide for themselves, thank her for making that difficult decision. The girls, who are also now in contact with their mother, concurred that their father was not a danger to them, but they would not have experienced any form of normalcy in their early lives had she carried on pursuing them.

When Aayesha was invited to share her story on a TV talk show, she clearly impressed the audience around the world with the amazing way she handled the situation. Other children who had experienced being abducted by their parents under various circumstances, lamented being put through the legal ordeal, all agreeing that Aayesha's way was by far the best in the given situations.

If a terribly hurt woman can collect herself, put aside her own grief, and decide to act in the best interests of her child, could international law not pluck a leaf or two off this emotional life lesson? Surely, the disintegration of parents' romantic relationship must not annihilate all traces of love among members of the affected family. Children must be allowed to live in an environment that highlights the true nature of both parents' love and affection towards them. The Hague Convention has the potential to create such an environment for families already facing a dilemma.

One of the most common reasons for child abductions seems to be linked to domestic violence or some other form of abuse. It would therefore be folly for the Hague Convention not to recognize this correlation. In addition, there are cases like Aayesha's where non-Convention countries are concerned.

Should the Convention remain silent and leave such parents to their own machinations simply because of technical jurisdiction matters? Certainly, this is an opportunity for the Convention to step in as the true international law it ought to be and bring the world closer to being the practical global village it strives to be.

The object of revising the Convention is rooted in

the attempt to build a good home for children caught in international divorces. The home, being a loving environment, should be provided by the parent who is most suitably placed to offer a nurturing environment for the children. This decision should not necessarily be motivated by prejudicial factors, such as cultural background, religion or social status. This is a matter of love, and love cannot be defined through such prejudices.

Rather than amplify technical matters, which can easily be abused, the Convention should focus on love. The reason is that no matter how much one can try, true love cannot be faked. It is either given or denied; expressed or withheld. But most of all, love is the only glue that cements the fragments of a broken family, even when they live away from each other. Once shared, love never really disintegrates. It will always exist and bring all parts of a family together, whether spiritually or physically.

That's why this love should be preserved at all costs. It is obvious in those cases that only one parent will get to spend more time with the children than the other. It should therefore be as accommodating as possible to the 'losing' parent, allowing them enough freedom to also have a chance to exercise their parental influence on their children. The focus should be on promoting the growth of love after the parents have separated from each other. Could there be anything more universal than love to solve such emotionally charged issues involving families and a law seeking relevance in a global village?

One of the worst problems veiling the free flow of love is discrimination based on race, religion, cultural beliefs and many other prejudicial factors. When cross cultural unions occur, it represents another step towards the attainment of a world free of such discriminatory elements. Such relationships create a fertile platform for the free exchange of cultural values, which effectively leads to better tolerance and understanding.

Centuries ago, such unions were simply unheard of, let alone comprehensible. The unspoken mantra encouraged people not to meddle with people and cultures they didn't understand. And that only worked to limit who certain people can interact with, exchange and share love with. But as people migrated throughout the world, the much-needed cultural exchanges created an exceptional opportunity for love to freely flow among and across the world's cultures. And that was a remarkable breakthrough in the world of love.

As the world's cultures mingle freely, intermarrying and procreating across each other, a new global citizen is born. One that is immune to the prejudices of the past and knows no segregation based on traditional prejudices. This is a huge leap in the advancement of human relations across the world. No longer is it totally taboo for a person to be involved in a relationship with someone who holds different beliefs, comes from a different culture or speaks a different language. Globalisation has done a lot to bring down the barriers, which seemed insurmountable only a few decades ago.

But like any other relationship, differences occur between individuals, leading to break-ups. Such differences should not be given a chance to be stereotyped into any form of representation of cultural differences. Instead, a love-based Convention would uphold the positives that exist between the individuals and the children involved, so that love continues to flow without any hard feelings.

The harder the Convention makes this break up, the worse the partners will feel towards each other; and the more likely they will develop prejudices. It is so unfortunate when such a thing happens, especially because the children are the ones left in the middle of the cultural differences. Being a product of the same two cultures, races or other difference which their feuding parents minimize to mere prejudices, they are left not knowing where to belong.

Take Matt as an example, an Australian who married a Japanese woman and had two sons while living in Australia. While Matt thought they were living a normal life as a family, his wife felt differently and she secretly wanted out. She told him that she missed home and needed to visit Japan with the children. Except, what Matt thought was his wife's home-sickness, was in fact a grand plan to take the children on a one-way ticket to her home country.

To no avail, Matt tried everything from legal proceedings in both Australia and Japan, to using his own connections to try and retrieve his two boys. Despite frequently travelling to Japan to see his children and paying for child support, his wife and mother-in-law still made it extremely difficult for Matt to see the boys and spend time with them. Understandably, Matt became very frustrated. But his frustration showed up in ways that also affected his children. The parents fell into the trap of involving the children in the bitter custody battle which ensued.

In one particular incident, Matt visited the children at their grandmother's house, intending to take them for the day as pre-arranged. But his mother-in-law would not allow him to, and his frustration turned into anger. An ugly scene resulted, in which one of his sons literally played referee in a heated verbal exchange between Matt and his mother-in-law. The adults hurled angry words at each other, while the boy tried to reason with his father to at least walk away and cool down.

Matt tried to explain to his young child how their mother and grandmother were being unfair to him by blocking his access to visiting them. It was tantamount to asking these innocent children to recognize their mother's ill-deeds, or asking them to see him as the good guy. The boy was clearly distraught, because two adults he probably respects equally made him the subject of their constant scuffles.

This incident had clearly created some kind of animosity not just between Matt and his wife. It also sucked in his mother-in-law and the whole Japanese society and system into the pool of bad guys who barred him from his children. Instead of Matt dealing with his problem with his wife, he seemed to generalize and blame everything Japanese for his problems. In an interview, Matt exclaimed, "...the legal system there is a farce... a blackhole for international abductions... that's a fact..."

No doubt, Matt deserved to feel the anger he felt during his ordeal. But he also demonstrated a personality which any parent in this situation has the potential to develop. It is highlighted by a tendency to paint everyone with the same brush, closing oneself within the narrow confines of a "them and us" mentality, which is contaminated by ugly prejudices towards those exhibiting different views.

What started as an expression of how much a father missed his sons, quickly degenerated into an ugly fight against a people. It will be difficult to witness a more desperate cry for a little more peace, tolerance and love from a child as young as Matt's son who was caught up when his own roots rose against each other. Honestly, where will such a child lean for emotional support and guidance when that which he relied on has revealed what can no longer be unseen? Surely, confusion and hurt shall enjoy a long abusive reign where love previously had a throne in his little heart.

The fact that a piece of legislation in the likes of the Hague Convention had to be crafted to regulate disputes following similar cross-cultural couples' breakups, is indeed a commendable initiative. At the least, it creates a platform upon which support can be provided in the most amicable manner, when disagreements do occur. But the world of love deserves far more than bare basics.

That's why an entire planet of love-filled souls is calling for a makeover of this international law, to make it more supportive, tolerant, all-inclusive and acceptable to all cultures of the world. When that small part is achieved, the world shall unleash a love that knows no limits. No longer will men and women hold back their love on the basis of trivial prejudices that have nothing to do with the dispensation of true love. The eruption of that brand-new kind of love is imminent!

CHAPTER 6:
WHAT PARENTS AND CHILDREN SIMPLY NEED

An Australian young woman in her mid-20's relates her childhood ordeal, which she suffered at the hand of her own mother. Though she seems quite composed, her voice expresses frustration while her demeanour reveals the grief she frantically tries to hide from the focus of those listening to her story.

Since Jo was only six years old, she vividly remembers how her mother told her that the two of them would be going on an adventure in Switzerland. It was supposed to be their little secret, which was to be kept from Daddy. This was probably an easy secret to keep because Jo's parents were divorced and she stayed with her mother; her dad only had her during weekends. But at the same time, she was confused about why she could not say goodbye to her father before leaving on this trip. However, she was too young to reason, and so she played this little silent part in her own abduction on Mummy's instructions.

She and her mum packed up and secretly left for Switzerland, leaving Jo's father in Australia to wonder what had happened to his ex-wife and daughter. Though she didn't know what was happening at the time, Jo remembered how her own mother planned and executed her abduction in such great detail. She even remembered how her mother made her choose a new name to go by during their stay in Switzerland, as well as the myriad of fairy tale promises she made to her about how great their new Swiss life would be.

Almost twenty years later, Jo does not only remember how her own abduction was carried out. She also recalls the difficulties her young self was subjected to during her short stay in Switzerland. She had no friends of her own age to play with. And she describes in detail how they lived in a small, dark studio apartment with her mother's strange partner, sleeping on the couch for over six months. Jo also remembers how her mum and her partner always used to fight. Worst of all, Jo remembers the horrible things her mother would constantly feed her young mind concerning her father.

Even as the young child she was then, Jo knew she was not at home in Switzerland, despite being with her mother. Jo missed the only home she knew. Australia was where she had made memories with both her mother and father. Australia was where she remembered having her last goodnight's sleep, in a decent bed. That's where familiar little kids were available to play with by day and there were no "stranger partner" in the house making her feel uneasy all the time. Although she was too young to make decisions for herself, she had a good idea who and what did not make her feel safe and loved.

The story of Jo is not necessarily about why her mother kidnapped her; or why her father went to such great lengths to retrieve her from halfway across the world. It is not about who was wrong or right, or who caused things to get so bad a child had to be taken from a decent home to a less comfortable place she did not like.

Yes, the Hague Convention is at the centre of this and many other child abduction cases which are happening daily. But the real driver of all these things is a simple need to love, be loved and express whatever beautiful thing comes out of such an exchange of emotions. The Convention and all its fancy rules are simply a peripheral situation which love needs to deal with.

Unfortunately, this ideal has been flipped on its head, and the Hague Convention has sought to snatch the reigns of international family relationships. As far as love is concerned, the Convention is way out of its league, seeking to resolve matters of the heart through means totally void of the requisite emotions.

To reconcile the Convention with the realities of international divorce and the dynamics of such family relationships in the aftermath of divorce, it is essential to consider what the affected family members need. By understanding each party's unique needs, the Convention can start to understand why certain actions occur.

At this level, the Convention can set feasible rules, which anyone can relate to when faced with similar circumstances. Unless this understanding is sought and grasped, it remains a near impossibility for the Convention to practically relate to situations on the ground. It is thus rendered an obsolete piece of legislation, which is inapplicable anywhere else outside of a law book.

First, let us take a look at the needs of children, those innocent souls at the core of the entire dispute, which motivated the birth of the Convention. The most basic of children's need is love, specifically parental love. Children's needs are unique because they not only lack the capacity, but also have no desire to set any preconditions for this need to be fulfilled. They choose neither parent nor sibling.

At the same time, they depend entirely on their parents to make important decisions about all aspects of their lives. As Bert Hellinger said in his book, *Love's Hidden Symmetry*, this is not a give and take relationship. Parents predominantly give to their children without expecting anything in return, otherwise the relationship is flawed.

Children, being the beautiful souls that they are, unequivocally accept both parents without any reservations. This has nothing to do with the parents' personality. Whether parents are cruel, loving, separated, divorced, living abroad or even completely absent from their lives, children still expect to be loved by their parents. This expectation is stimulated by the fact that they already love their parents, and expect their parents to reciprocate unconditionally.

As previously discussed, children require a home. Wherever they feel loved and well provided for, children associate that place with their ideal home. Because a true home is not merely a place, parents are expected by their children to provide more emotional resources, such as quality time, encouragement and protection.

The rest of the things parents provide, such as the quality of the physical house, clothes, food, and so on are just aesthetics. This explains why some of the richest people in the world can fail to provide a proper home for their children, or children from affluent families run away to stay happily in a shack, which is filled with more love than gifts totally devoid of sentiment. This is what children basically need, and it is not negotiable. Whether you give it to them or not and how much of it you offer, will determine the quality of parent one becomes.

Adults can only wish their needs were half as simple as their children's. As a parent, you have to balance your personal, family and partner's needs, in addition to attending to your children's needs. All of these classes of needs are super important to every responsible parent, otherwise cracks begin to appear in those relationships receiving the least attention. What further complicates this needs matrix in relation to the Hague Convention is that they demand more attention when there is divorce in the family.

As a consequence of divorce, each parent naturally focuses on the children, as evidenced by the custody discussions which punctuate most divorce settlements. A mother desperately needs to nurture the spiritual bond which started forming during her pregnancy and has thrived with each day their child grows. Meanwhile, a father makes every attempt to prolong his progress towards stamping his position as an important person of influence in various aspects of the child's life.

Both parents completely understand what divorce

means to their relationship with the children. Precisely, parents suddenly realize that they have to give up at least some of their time with the children, which essentially means they have limited time to impress all their love upon the children's hearts. Time with the children, which was previously taken for granted, suddenly becomes an excruciatingly scarce resource. This is the dilemma of every divorcing parent.

On another level, each parent develops needs which only the other parent can fulfil. As long as they are going to share time with the children, parents continue to need each other. Each one feels they are giving away a part of themselves when children go away to the other parent. That means each parent needs the other to be responsible enough to take good care of the children. They can no longer share this responsibility as each one takes responsibility for the time he or she is with the children. And each one needs to trust the other that they will stick to the agreed visitation schedule.

This is the part where the Hague Convention is required to regulate sticky points. Past experiences with each other, reasons for break-up, and other unresolved issues make valid reasons for such needs to remain unfulfilled. In most cases, bad blood simply blocks out any chances of partners fulfilling these needs for each other. Take the case involving a partner with a history of abuse – can they be trusted to be alone with the children? As long as the other partner feels that their ex is not capable of creating a conducive home for the children, they will struggle to cooperate with whatever law or person who tries to force them otherwise.

In addition, parents' personal needs do not suddenly diminish because of a divorce. In fact, each parent wants to prove (whether to themselves or others) that they can look after the children well by taking good care of themselves. A life falling apart has never made a great case for a custody battle. The natural feeling is that if one cannot take care of themselves, how can they take on the responsibility of taking care of others? This is one of the most common challenges faced by women seeking to return to their home country with their children.

If we revisit Sarah's situation where she has to depend on Eddie as long as she is in the UK, we will better understand why this is so. Such parents are not only seeking a return to their countries; they are seeking to meet a deeper need to restore their independence, especially if they are coming out of an abusive relationship.

If the Hague Convention is to make any real contribution to international relationships, it should aim beyond simply settling legal disputes. It should be re-designed to address the deeper issues affecting restoration of lost love, re-building of crumbling relationships and providing a platform upon which family relationships can flourish, even in the aftermath of divorce. The Convention is a law affecting more than individuals. Its effects have far-reaching consequences which will be felt generations later. To make any impact, the Convention must first seek to have relevance where it seeks to be applied. Since it works within the confines of family relationships, which are largely shaped by emotions, it is best that it applies solutions that have more emotion than legal technicality.

When parents divorce, they should understand that even if they are granted custody, it does not necessarily make them the "preferred parent." To their children, they are still Mom or Dad and both needed for exclusive roles. It is important that parents who take the children understand their children's need to continue interacting with the other parent. Whether this need is fulfilled through supervised visits or other visitation arrangements, it is important that there are feasible options available to consider. When the Convention creates an unfair advantage for one parent in this regard, it ceases to be relevant and therefore loses its credibility. Parents will react impulsively, leading to unfortunate situations, such as parental abductions, alienation and other ugly scuffles.

One of the worst developments that have sprung out of desperate Hague Convention situations is an unusual business service offering international retrieval of abducted children. Besides the unfortunate attempt to profit out of such sensitive matters, such services have the potential to cause even more harm to children. They use unspecified means to retrieve children who have been taken to non-Convention countries, including illegal and potentially dangerous methods. In addition, such services are clearly no different to the original abduction. They inflict the same traumatic effects on the child as the original abduction. Jo and others who experienced being abducted by a parent openly confess what horror it is. One can only imagine how a child would feel if they had to be re-abducted; this time by a total stranger. The psychological trauma is beyond imagination.

Although the Convention may not directly deal with such business services, it can help reduce demand for such services by addressing the underlying needs which parents seek to meet through those services. Businesses that try to find legal loopholes and orchestrate re-abduction of children to a non-Convention country, are illegal, and technically, should be banned.

Finally, both parents and children involved in international divorce need healing. This is perhaps the most important of their needs. Though it may hurt for a while, each member of such families looks forward to the day when they can move on to a new chapter of their lives. Children want to ease into the idea of not living with both parents, and learn to understand how they can best relate to each parent during the limited time they are available.

On the other hand, either parent needs to find a new path and discover how their children, ex-partner and new relationships can work together going forward. The Convention would have failed if it does not help to mend the hearts of broken families, especially the children. But it is also important to note that meeting the children's needs naturally takes care of the bulk of parents' needs, because children are right at the centre of what each parent needs.

CHAPTER 7:
THERE ARE THREE SIDES TO THIS STORY

When Laura Garett ran off to Australia with her four daughters, she justified her actions by telling the world a sad story of domestic abuse by her husband. Laura's mother also alleged that Tomasso, Laura's Italian husband, was possibly sexually abusive to the girls. Besides being part of a plan to alienate Tomasso, these accusations simply raised questions around the kind of person, husband and father Tomasso is.

But speaking to Tomasso, the face of this Hague Convention story suddenly changed to that of deceit, conspiracy and shady conduct on the part of Laura and her mother. When the Vincenti girls were violently taken from their mother in Australia and forced onto a plane back to Italy, Laura painted a gloomy picture which showed herself as a distraught mother who has lost her girls' custody to an abusive foreign partner.

As events unfolded, stories of Laura's alleged extra-marital affairs, her mother's abuse of Tomasso's property, an attempt to re-abduct the kids and Australian Embassy

Staff's involvement created doubt about the truthfulness of Laura's account. Such is the veil casted over by litigation. Instead of sticking to evidence a claim or defend against it, both parties end up bringing much more into the courtroom than is necessary, in order to discredit the other and cast doubt. So instead of evidencing and mitigating risks, potentially too much noise drags cases on, adding to the wounds instead of preventing further hurt so healing can begin.

A certain lawyer shared an interesting analysis, which I found pretty interesting, as a general way to look at cases brought before the courts. He says whenever he gets a client who wants to sue a foe, he tells the person, "…there are potentially three sides to your case – yours, your foe's and THE TRUTH." This lawyer claims that this has held true for just about every case he's dealt with. Indeed, The Truth, in the eyes of the law, for each person has his or her own human truth based upon perspective, that may not necessarily be aligned with their higher Truth.

But the Hague Convention cases are somewhat different. Though a ruling may be in favour of one parent, it does not quite feel like a win. Few of the parents walk away with everything they want, particularly because a divorce always leaves a void in all family members' lives. The divorce process mediated by the courts simply tries to create a soft landing for all parties. But they are all landing after a mighty fall, which is always going to leave them with scars, bruises and broken limbs.

This is why everyone affected by a divorce needs time to heal and find a new path to their life's destiny. And like any other legal process, representations are made from both feuding parties, each trying to position themselves for a favourable ruling. In the process, truths, untruths and half-truths are uncovered and revealed, further widening rifts between relationships and deepening the need for healing. Just like my lawyer friend's professional motto, the Hague Convention should also recognize that each Convention case has three definite sides to it. But unlike general legal cases, Convention cases should look at these sides to the story in a different way.

FIRST DIMENSION

Every case must evaluate things through the eyes of a child who stands at the centre of his or her parents' breakup. If there are any victims in divorce cases, they can only be children. Parents actively decide to step onto that path, but children have absolutely no say in the one thing that can alter their life path significantly.

In addition to their struggle to acclimatize to their new life with only one parent (or in some cases, plus a parent's new partner), children often have a hard time figuring out how to deal with a myriad of mixed feelings. It is confusing to witness these two important people, called parents, going at each other's throats during court proceedings. It is particularly stressful when parents decide not to remain civil to each other for the sake of the children. It gets even worse when parent alienation is thrown into the mix; children start wondering whether they are truly loved or they are just some kind of means to a convenient end for whoever gets them between Mom and Dad.

Most Hague Convention stories are told from the parents' perspective. Parents go on about how they are at risk of losing touch with their children and express their deepest worries about their children's welfare. Each parent who tells their story almost always tries to justify why the children are worse off with the other parent. Whether or not that is the truth, there is a dimension which is always taken for granted.

The Convention itself imposes a habitual residence based on purely technical reasons. Parents no doubt want custody out of love for their children, in most cases. But that "love for child" completely ignores the children's feelings about everything that's happening.

Aayesha's response to her children's abduction to Morocco is heroic, in a big way. Instead of pursuing her husband and retrieving her children as she was legally supposed to; she simply considered what the children would go through and decided to retreat. It was a painful decision; even one that many would consider highly controversial.

The bottom line is this: not everything is black and white in these cases, even what's 'right' is not always the 'best' way around Hague Convention cases. Out of anger, frustration and many other circumstances, parents may fail to agree on what is best for the children. The Hague Convention should therefore step in as an impartial mediation tool, which stands for children's best interests. But it can only do so if it rids itself of its many flaws, which literally expose children to irreversible psychological damages.

THE SECOND DIMENSION

After all the fights, verbal exchanges and emotional battering, only one parent will emerge as the primary guardian for the children. This comes as a result of either a ruling of a court process, or an illegal removal of children from the country, also known as parental abduction. Unfortunately, though the latter is not in the least condoned, it is a reality that must be recognized as a way in which desperate parents are snatching primary guardianship in international divorces. But that's not the focus point at this time; the parent who loses custody is.

In abduction cases, they call this parent "The Left Behind Parent." In legal proceedings, this is the parent who has to deal with the possibility of the primary guardian legally leaving the country with the children. Either way, this means that the parent's time with the children is, at best, highly limited. First off, when children are abducted, the left behind parent should brace for the worst, never seeing their children again.

This is particularly the case when children are abducted to a non-Convention country where retrieval is not possible through legal means. On the other hand, when the Convention gives its blessing for a parent to leave the country with the children, the other parent faces huge travelling expenses if they want to see their children. But the financial cost is nothing compared to the anguish the left-behind parents feel.

Not having convenient and free access to children is pure torture for any good parent. A parent who knows and respects their responsibilities as a parent knows that losing the children means losing a chance to influence them towards what is deemed good.

Equally, the parent living with the children will also want to influence them towards the same goal, and every healthy parent knows that two healthy parents are always better than one (all being equal, of course!). Where traces of parental alienation exist in the case, the left behind parent's anguish exponentially escalates. Imagine not only being away from your children, but also facing the possibility of them growing up thinking you never cared about them.

These are some of the pertinent issues which the Hague Convention should address. Whatever ruling it makes must recognize that the parent who loses custody still remains the child's parent. A father or mother does not cease to be one after the case has concluded.

In fact, they need a chance to become more of a parent thereafter, in order to keep the flame of their family love alight. A revised Convention should restore the hope of these parents, give them a chance to restore and maintain relations with their absent children, and forge new alliances with their ex-partners which ultimately benefit the children's up-bringing.

THE THIRD DIMENSION

Finally, the Convention should explore what would typically go on in the life of the parent who either abducts a child or wins legal custody and leaves the country with the children. Just like the left-behind parent does not become less of a parent, neither does the primary guardian become more of a parent through attainment of custody, care and control.

As such, a revised Convention should explore ways in which international parents can be guided around access to children through scheduled visits. The frustration of trying to go through foreign legal systems is not a secret. It drove Matt into anger-charged arguments with his wife and mother-in-law when he felt they were barring his visits in Japan. The same frustration drove Aayesha to the most important decision of her life, after realizing that her husband would never settle with the children as long as her legal pursuit lasted.

In addition, a revised Convention should take massive steps to create conditions which nullify the need to resort to abduction. Currently, the majority of abductions are largely a result of parents finding the process tipped against what is right. For example, abusive partners taking advantage of technicalities to prevent their victims from leaving with the children.

Failure to address these grey areas means the world will continue to deal with the ghosts of parental abductions, motivated by the urge to escape to freedom with their children. This also means hurt for the children. Like Aayesha's husband in Morocco and Jo's mother in Switzerland, the abducting parent will stay on the run from the law, denying the children the stability they need to lead normal lives.

All Hague Convention cases, whatever their specific details, have to deal with issues from these three dimensions. Failure to recognize these dimensions means failure to address the needs of all parties involved in the divorce. Ultimately, it means divorced families either take longer to heal, or they never do, which would be an unfortunate tragedy.

But the world, in the magnificent glory of love, knows no failure. Humanity cannot afford to fail at loving; the consequences are too dire to contemplate. Love shall prevail, and love shall conquer, as it always does. Relationships shall flourish again, even after the devastating blows of international divorce. The Hague Convention shall be revised to restore hope for a true global village in which the union of cultures continues to bear ambassadors of a purer form of love.

Arise humanity, the dawn of new love beckons!

REFERENCES AND FURTHER READING

https://www.youtube.com/watch?v=HwqzZjoKgok&t=977s

https://nationalparentsorganization.org/blog/22278-the-tommaso-vincenti-case-his-daughters-speak-out

http://www.dailymail.co.uk/news/article-3035362/How-four-sisters-dragged-kicking-screaming-Australian-mother-sent-monster-Italian-father-learnt-cope-traumatic-ordeal-regret-behaved.html

http://www.smh.com.au/national/vincenti-sisters-reveal-what-it-was-like-to-be-taken-from-australia-back-to-italy-20150411-1mj7bb.html

https://www.youtube.com/watch?v=aeWiy4T_lZU&t=1000s

https://www.youtube.com/watch?v=o4Qh_PF9rW0&t=129s

http://www.economist.com/news/international/21716991-parents-can-face-lengthy-court-battles-or-become-permanently-estranged-their

https://www.youtube.com/watch?v=BBmiiyfOFmw

https://www.youtube.com/watch?v=Xgk3XAJ5TQk

http://www.globalarrk.org/globalarrk-statistics

http://www.mychildmagazine.com.au/the-expats-tale-im-a-stuck-mum/

http://www.seychellesmama.com/raising-awareness-expat-stuck-parent/

https://www.theguardian.com/lifeandstyle/2015/may/16/the-mothers-fighting-to-get-their-children-back-home-again

http://www.straitstimes.com/singapore/uber-mum-driven-to-make-kids-lives-easier

http://www.telegraph.co.uk/expat/expatnews/9550557/How-international-issues-further-complicated-child-custody-cases.html

http://www.divorcenet.com/states/nationwide/child_custody_international_moves

http://kenyalaw.org/newsletter/20110701.html

http://www.marilynstowe.co.uk/2010/05/28/expat-divorce-forum-shopping/

http://www.forbes.com/sites/jefflanders/2013/01/10/small-world-big-problem-divorces-involving-dual-citizenship/#5fb0e0875391

https://www.youtube.com/watch?v=FZ20YMhGHCY

PART 3:
MANIFESTING WITH LOVE

CHAPTER 8:
IN PRACTICE

The official document describes The Hague Convention in the following way:

The principal object of the Convention, aside from protecting rights of access, is to protect children from the harmful effects of cross-border abductions (and wrongful retentions) by providing a procedure designed to bring about the prompt return of such children to the State of their habitual residence. The Convention is based on a presumption that, save in exceptional circumstances, the **wrongful removal or retention** *of a child across international boundaries is not in the interests of the child, and that the return of the child to the State of the habitual residence will promote his or her interests by vindicating the* **right of the child to have contact with both parents***, by supporting* **continuity in the child's life***, and by ensuring that any determination of the issue of custody or access is made by the most appropriate court having regard to the likely availability of relevant evidence. The principle of prompt return also serves as a deterrent to abductions and wrongful removals,* *and this is seen by the Convention to be in the interests of children generally.* **The return order is designed to restore the status quo which existed before the wrongful removal or protection, and to deprive the wrongful parent of any advantage that might otherwise be gained by the abduction.**

Reference: https://assets.hcch.net/docs/e6a6a977-40c5-47b2-a380-b4ec3a0041a8.pdf

The grey area consists of the following:
- what could be deemed *wrongful removal* could also not be deemed as such, given certain factual differences for each case.
- when there is a divorce taking place, *continuity* in the form it was prior to the divorce process kicking off no longer exist but a Hague return does not require prior agreement as to how living or access arrangements would be in the interim.
- such *contact* differs from family to family, not to mention that in an increasingly technologically connected world, while never a substitute for physical contact, virtual video contact is still contact.
- *to deprive the wrongful parent of any advantage* could sound simplistic, arrogant, and biased, to the lay person reading it.

For every Left-Behind Parent, there is a Stuck Parent. GlobalARRK is an international charity specialising in helping 'stuck parents.' A stuck parent is a parent who, after moving abroad followed by a relationship breakdown, is unable to return to their home country with their children or is forced to be separated from them because they are unable to remain in that country together.

Either way you look at it, there is a child who defines home with feelings of love and safety, and this is not accounted for in the Hague Convention. The pitfalls that come from the notion of habitual residence ought to make it irrelevant in the determinant of the court order, and perhaps instead, immediately accelerate the case into an alternative family dispute resolution process. Every case is unique, and putting a time stamp regardless whether it is as short as one week to as long as five years for a child to be considered habitually resident and cannot return home with the primary carer, especially when he/she gets care and control, is unfair to everyone in the eyes of love even if it looks fair in the eyes of the law.

Removal without consent is different from abduction, and therefore needs to be handled with greater respect and sensitivity to the whole family because a family is a family no matter what. In regards to arguments on equal parental involvement, the law is making a huge assumption and imposing a blanket value system and approach as to what and how parental involvement should look like for ALL families, dismissing that every family is different, every child is different, and every person has his/her own journey.

Any law reformation calls for fair representation in the committee responsible for the reformation, and by fair, I do not mean an equal split in the parental gender representation of, but also include individuals who can hold the space to catalyse change in diverse and complex

Love with Passion and Perspective

cross-border situations. The Hague Convention cannot be reformed through debate alone, if it is to bring about sustainable change through shifting behaviours in the long run. We have seen the flaws of voting systems and political campaigns... the Hague Convention can lead the way in promoting the restoration of systemic health because the family system is where everything begins.

Everything changes when we put family love first and foremost. If we simply aim to govern behaviours through the law and let fear take leadership, we are limiting and hindering the true capacity and power of the law to raise the game. More controls and policing does not tend to raise the game. Instead it encourages manipulation through finding loopholes where alternative dispute resolution would have greater potential to encompass every situation possible while avoiding the casualties of litigation.

My 4-year-old's book *The Lion Inside* contains a quote:

"If you want things to change, you first have to change YOU."

The meaning of this quote is profound. The link between what we want to change that is outside of our immediate control, and changing ourselves, is not always crystal clear, especially when we are in the thick of it all.

As Hillary Munyoro reflected, when we use the law to govern Family Love, without supporting the processes for love to flow, before, during and after the breakup, the collective price paid in the form of systemic pain is significant and extends beyond the immediate generation.

The more we allow fear to lead the way, even if it is

to flee horrible domestic violence situations, the more we apply resistance to what we want and the more we actually permit what we do not want to infiltrate our experience.

When Love leads the way and the human fear simply left there to exist and come to pass, the better we heal from any trauma brought about through the divorce process, and the greater the likelihood of being truly and deeply heard.

At the time of writing, GlobalARRK is preparing a petition with several proposals that will bring the Hague Convention slightly more up-to-date. They also have on their website, a pre-emigration order that every relocating family ought to know about.

Reference:
http://www.globalarrk.org/amend-the-hague-october-2017

THE ALTERNATIVE

When I chose to walk the road of divorce, I got to know my fears much more intimately than I ever would. I got a chance to face them with all the fears running wild within and watch them melt away, in part like illusion, and in another part, countered by my growing capacity, for when I recognised my capacity to hold the inner tension that came with facing my fears, my expanded capacity became realised and relative to that, the fear could not exist in the same way.

Perhaps my experience, learning and insight would have been very different if my legal situation was fed by deep pockets. As neither of us were in a practical position

Love with Passion and Perspective

to litigate, and I was so far from desiring any litigation, we learnt to step up and find alternative ways to come to an agreement for a way forward.

Many whom I spoke to have experienced the legal system as a battlefield where there is lawful play, but not necessarily fair play. Lawful play means covering bases, killing the opponent so long as one follows the rule, finding loopholes and manipulating the actors in court with sophisticated psychological tactics. Therefore, while I do believe that the law can serve and protect many, the law has its limits, and the law cannot change human behaviour in a sustainable way. A legal case has a punitive tone to it even as it aims to protect and it brings out in full force the shadow side of human behaviour that have long-standing negative impact, chiefly victimhood and vindictiveness.

I found my legal counsel from another lawyer who (unethically) taught me to write to all the expat lawyers and approach them so that they will not be able represent my ex. The good news for me was that I could read up on them all, and approached to get a sense for how they are. Several were money-oriented, some were completely run by inexperienced lawyers, one of which even asked me to pay $700 for the 45-minute call with her instead of the lawyer I asked for, **<u>after</u>** the call was done, and I gained absolutely nothing from her compared to some other lawyers whom I spoke to before and after her at no charge!

Helen Chia was my legal counsel. There was something about her from the first meeting and although we have had our hiccups during the legal process, she had always been there for me. Her interest in Alternative Dispute Resolution only become apparent to me after my case was effectively closed, even though she had mentioned it right from the start.

I was blessed that my ex multiplied his efforts to look at the bigger picture and think differently for within three months, we managed to deal with our disputes at the family courts mediation, without needing to engage private support. Post closure of my case, I began talking to Helen about her passion in Alternative Dispute Resolution as the founder of Trinity ADR.

Helen's journey to setting up the company was multifaceted; from personal experience in dealing with her legal work, inspiration from formal training, and putting into practice alternative forms of dispute resolution as a way of life. Part of her journey included meeting a crisis on one of her cases that involved the death of a child whilst in the care of one of the parents in the midst of a stressful custody battle and a year on, on a separate case, a client was brutally injured. It was in this vein that Helen started to question the deeper need to amalgamate various forms of Alternative Dispute Resolution and all social support for a family in crisis.

It was on the back of the first crisis that the company was founded. The occurrence of the second crisis sealed the resolve to ensure that the vision and reach of her work would be available to all. Their uniqueness lies in the integrated and holistic approach taken to cater to the full spectrum of needs with specialists in general mediation, family mediation including parental child abduction under the Hague Convention, negotiation, arbitration, counselling and psychological care for family and children, as well as workshops to fill the gap in starting any healing process.

There is always an alternative. But one can only receive its benefits if these alternatives are understood and an informed choice is made on how to move on.

It is my personal belief that everything happens FOR me, and I believe that I receive gifts upon gifts from any experience that I deemed painful. But as mentioned before, it is not that therefore the structures, constructs, design and law should remain as it is. I believe that where shifts had been made out of the pains of others who courageously spoke up, it is so that we are well ready to be with other experiences and keep up with living our dreams in different, more expansive ways.

I am grateful to have come to know Dr Nancy Sutton-Pierce as I practiced the vibrations of my being that had expanded from the gifts of my life journey. Nancy embodies alignment and oozes confidences and love, and she is such because of her ability to love all parts of her, deeply, consciously, and compassionately, so much so that what she carries with her inspires movements and cuts through fogginess in the matrix.

I asked her to contribute from her heart to this next segment, so you will experience her energy as well. I hope it will add to the light illuminating your path forward in life.

PEARLS OF TRAUMA

My professional background is of a registered nurse and health educator. I went from being an obstetrics nurse where I helped to birth babies, to running an outpatient clinic and taking care of thousands of people with diabetes over a 30-year span.

I got into yoga by accident through my daughters about 23 years ago and that opened my eyes to a whole new way of thinking, feeling and being in my body and my life that has continued to evolve and change many aspects of it.

I also opened up to human sexuality and relationships, and I found myself going back to school, at the age of 58, and getting my doctorate degree in human sexuality. Now I am a clinical sexologist and educator around the world. So I bring forward all these aspects of my career in nursing and health education into yoga, human sexuality, and relationships.

As I move through life, I increasingly realize that the story we tell ourselves about our past has a humongous influence on our present. And so I'm going to share with you my story and] give you some details that may be uncomfortable for me to see in print.

As an infant, I was placed for adoption. My birth mother was 16 at that time and courageously put me up for adoption because she knew she could not take care of me. I was adopted by a loving family who had waited 12 years to get me. I grew up knowing I was adopted and I felt very loved and wanted by my adoptive parents. I was known as "the adopted darling." My parents were hard workers and did their best but they had their struggles. They were both alcoholics. At 5 o'clock every evening, they would go from sober to drunk, and when that happened, they disappeared. Physically, they were there, but I felt alone and abandoned.

I had a brother who is nine years older who sexually molested me when I was seven or eight years old. At the time, I did not really understand what was going on. I just knew he was doing things to me that were secret. I did not feel assaulted but I knew our actions would not be approved of by our parents. I never told my parents about this. The sexual molestation went on for a couple of years, and it impacted me in a big way.

I was very curious about sexuality from my early teens. I was sexually active at the age of 14 and got married to my high school boyfriend at the age of 17. Four years later we had a daughter. During those years I did not know who I was. I knew I wanted to be a nurse. I knew I wanted to have a career in the health professions, but I did not understand my value as a human being and as a woman. My husband then was abusive verbally and emotionally. He always made me seem to be the crazy one in the relationship. I think we call that gaslighting now.

He tried hard to manipulate me into doing what he wanted me to do. After giving birth to my daughter and having this child that I was responsible for, I became hyper aware of the influence that our relationship, our interaction, and his force was having on her. Eventually, when my daughter was three, after two episodes of physical abuse, I managed to leave. It took me two years.

I found this path of passion for engaging with women around the world who were struggling with the same thing I had been struggling with. I found very little support from my own family. My sister-in-law and my mom believed that once you get married, you are supposed to stay married forever, and because I initiated the divorce, I was the bad one.

By doing the hard thing, I had to keep it in mind that I was demonstrating to my daughter that not only will there be days when you have to make tough choices, but also how important it is for us as women and men to grow and mature and know ourselves well enough before we choose a partner. Had I been mature and confident and understood my self-worth then I most likely wouldn't have chosen the partner I did.

My story is what I was. What were the things that I needed to create in my life to learn the lessons I have learned? It is not who I am today. Who I am today can remember those things and remember the feelings I had going through them, but I am not a victim. I can look at every piece of my story growing up and see a pearl that helped me move into the next phase of my life... beyond the trauma, beyond the conditions.

As we recap our stories, it is important we are able to not look at ourselves as victims but as students. We were presented with opportunities in order to learn valuable lessons. Did we learn them? And are we taking what we have learned and moving forward in our own lives? That's something we can do on a daily basis.

After my divorce, I continued my education. I had a great career and about ten years later I married the man of my dreams. Through him, our relationship and how we work together, I learned several more lessons. But I do not know that I would have been prepared to learn those lessons had I not lived through the ones before. Therefore, I do not second guess my early story. I look at it with gratitude and appreciation because if it were not for all of those things, I would not be who I am today, and who I am today is pretty awesome.

I share that with you so you can see that you and I have a lot in common. It does not matter that I was born in California, USA, or you are born in another country. We are spiritual beings on our human journey. We may have different details, but we all can share the same story. We can inspire each other to know how to move forward.

No matter where you live, culture and beliefs have influenced us. They have influenced men and their roles and attitudes and they have influenced women in the same way . So, we have to be mindful when we are faced with these choices and decisions that we see the big picture and we carry the torch of positivity and loving-kindness forward, no matter how we were treated.

I have spoken to men and women around the

world, and both genders have had trauma. Both genders have been treated in unfavourable ways. We all have our story. What is most important is that we are able to recognize how our story is influencing who we are right now. Am I better? Am I encouraged? Am I strong? Am I a victim? Am I revengeful?

Taking my story as an example, how am I using it to live my life today? Am I using it as an excuse to mistreat others or did I spin it and understand compassionately and empathetically how that is not how I would ever want to treat another being? And so, I learnt, I have the pearl, and I hold onto that pearl.

However, it is hard to remember that when we are stuck in our story in a negative spin. I challenge you to look at your story with a positive attitude and find the pearls. Find the lessons that were presented to you to learn. As women, our daughters, our sisters, our mothers, our friends are all watching us. We are walking role models whether we want to be or not. I have three daughters, two daughters and a daughter-in-law, plus four granddaughters. So in my inner family alone, I have six women watching me to see how I conduct myself, how I use my story, and how I treat others.

We are all being watched, so we get to start the example rather than be the warning. For example, there is something called slut shaming, where when women are expressing their sexuality, their comfort in their skin, their freedom, their spontaneity, their liberation, oftentimes we view that as a threat, as a *negative insult and we condemn them because they are not living up to the standard we still buy into. Girls or ladies do not act that way. When you hear yourself putting another person down, please pause.*

Think about where your belief has come from. Has it been instilled upon you by how you have been treated, and if so, how did that feel? Did you feel supported or worried? Did you feel loved? Did you feel appreciated. Did you feel that you are free to express and explore who you were authentically meant to be? Or are you still living in that box that somebody somewhere put you in?

I am a freethinker, a free spirit, and yet I have had to work hard to find those moments when I was tempted to fall back into the old beliefs, into old ways of thinking, and speak about women in a favourable way. I learned a lot, including that my gift to women is to support them.

It is to create a space for them. I do not need to challenge them, I do not need to condemn them, and I do not need to condone them, because truly it is not my place to do any of those. It is simply my place to hold the space for any women I am with to be authentically who they are and embrace that. I like to imagine a world where all people were treated that way. So, when you speak to your daughters about how you dress, behave or present yourself, be mindful.

Are you encouraging her to live from the heart place? Are you encouraging her to really be free? To do and behave in ways that make her feel alive, vibrant, excited, and enthusiastic about her life? Because that is the only way we should be encouraging her: to live from that true authentic place within. When she does that, she will feel free, she will feel strong, she will feel powerful. Feeling this way, what kind of life partner will she attract? A partner who loves that or tries to change it? Chances are, if she is standing firmly in her own power, the only people who will be drawn to her are the people who want to bask in her light, not dim it.

Let's bring forward the pearls and then look at our pearls every day and we say, "What am I going to do with these pearls today?" How am I going to make my life more adventurous, more exciting, more wonderful, more loving? And how can I share these pearls with everybody else I know? How do we take our story, infuse it into who we are today, and then move it forward?

Everything I teach has to do with consciousness. My yoga studio is called Conscious Living Yoga. I teach conscious living sexuality. I have a radio show called The Conscious Living show. One of the most important aspects of consciousness is how we talk to ourselves. That inner dialogue going on 24/7 which creates the reality we are living today and that is going to create the reality we live tomorrow.

As we step out into the world to make a big change, it needs to start inside with who we are right now. Pay attention to how you speak to yourself. One of the tools I teach is journaling, where you free write

Love with Passion and Perspective

what you are thinking, what you are feeling, what is going on in your life. You write for maybe five minutes every day and then you look back to circle the words you see a lot.

You will find a thread of consciousness come through your writing. The words you are speaking to yourself are imparting an attitude and a self-perception that you show to the world. If you are always saying things like 'I am learning', 'I am excited', 'I am happy', 'this is fun', 'that is sexy' etc, or if those inner dialogues are negative, victimized, unsupportive, condemning, fearful, shameful, then that is the reality you will be living. If we want to change our reality, it has to come from how we are thinking.

Become conscious of how you are thinking and look for the thread. Is it positive? Is it lifting you up or tearing you down? And if it's tearing you down then go back through your writing and scratch out the words that are harmful to you, dehumanizing, diminishing... and replace them with words that are uplifting, supportive, loving, and kind. And then reread that story every day. Surround yourself with this new consciousness and watch the miracles that unfold for you.

I teach yoga as a therapy program and one of the tasks I set is for everybody to write their story and speak to the class. Then I say, "That's the last time you will tell that story because your story begins today. You take those pearls, you take your consciousness, and you rewrite your story every day that you wake up."

You get to decide your story. Is it going to be a story of success, love, passion, excitement, enthusiasm, learning, growing, expanding and all those wonderful things that we all desire and deserve? Or is it going to be something else? It's up to you. It's up to me. The only person that I really get to influence on how it goes from here, is me. I also get to watch other people and use their example-ness or their warning-ness. I can learn from that a little bit but truly what is going on in my heart and gut, is my greatest teacher.

One of the most powerful tools in yoga to listen to your heart's desire is to get quiet, get grounded, take a breath, and think about the sentence:

My deepest heartfelt desire is... The answer usually comes fast. It will generally pop up like a vision or an image.

We may find ourselves saying or thinking, "Oh I can't have that, I don't deserve that. Oh no, no, not that, how embarrassing, how wrong." Or we might say or think, "I want to be sexy, I want to be delicious, I want to be honouring, I want to be adventurous." That is your heart speaking. That is your truth. That is where you live. And when you try to shut that up, everything shuts down. Your excitement about life. Your physical energy, your sexual energy, your creative energy... it all gets squelched until you feel dead inside.

As a nurse and a health educator I have worked long enough in my career over 30 years to know that women in their 40s, 50s and 60s, who have been conditioned or have conditioned themselves to shut all that down, feel tired, dead and burdened. They are not excited about the next phase. They do not look forward to creating something new.

We can change that right here and right now. We have the power to shift our thinking. It is simply a matter of turning that light bulb on and deciding. Let it be beyond your wildest dreams. Let it move your imagination to outer boundaries. When we can let this go, then we are truly examples of living in the full illuminated light that we are. And imagine that your daughter or your sister or your mom or the women that you know, your girlfriends and the men, all benefit tremendously from you shining to your full capacity."

CHAPTER 9:
VIBRATING YOUR DREAM

Imagine a world without shame or guilt. Imagine overcoming the ultimate of all fears – the fear of death. How do you allow yourself to be that? How do you vibrate that?

A world with no narcissism, no co-dependency, no abuse... and what holds out and holds space is ultimate potentiality. To dance with the inner guide... to trust in one's own readiness to see what is ordinarily, unknowingly, avoided... to swim beyond the depths of the ocean... to touch the different openings, not knowing what it unravels yet knowing nonetheless because what attracts is that which is likened to itself... there is no way of getting it wrong, no end to the movement of the energy, to the transformation... until it transmutes on its return to pure potentiality.

To have visions and to know them as vibrational information... never personal. To feel the pain of all women, to know the source of the fire and light within, to allow the elements and the unseen to guide, to surrender to the inner guidance that leads creation, to live and work as the magician and the fool where

Love with Passion and Perspective

> *the world is you in pure potentiality.*
> *What is it like to truly embody that which you*
> *are? To embody a Universe?*
> *It is a dream. It is a dream come true.*
>
> — **Adele M Lim**

That was the message from my inner guidance that I received during my last innerdance session in which Pi facilitated before he killed off his online profile and entered his second hermitage.

That innerdance translates into an outerdance that re-informs the innerdance that then gets translated again into an outerdance, in infinitesimal loops. The processes have brought me to alignment and realignment, emergence and convergence, and with a sense of knowingness in the unknown.

The law of attraction and the law of resonance supported the grounding of my expansion. I fell in love with the world, just as I fell in love with nothingness. There is simplicity in satisfaction and contentment in action or inaction that defies time and space into beauty. This realisation would not have been possible without the vastness experienced through self-discovery tools that brought me to sense cosmic space to bring into being, what was dreamed up.

Every time I affirm that I am right where I need to be at this point in time, my discomfort tells me about the missing piece and lets me know that I can fulfil myself regardless of the external conditions. This helps me let go of negative emotions and resistances, releasing me in the direction of my desires. The journey reminds me of my nature and as I lean towards compliments and tune into what I want instead of what I do not want, I am tuning into a future that is the highest version of my dreams as opposed to a future that looks like the past.

Every person will have their own reality. I have no right to control or attempt to change that. The one thing I can do is to role model liberation, to role model freedom, to role model responsibility, i.e. response-ability. Being adult means skilful handling of what once overwhelmed the inner child, and accepting another person's reality with no judgment or fear.

Yogi Bhajan issued five sutras for the Aquarian Age:
1. Recognise that the other person is you.
2. When the time is on you, start, and the pressure will be off.
3. Vibrate the cosmos; the cosmos shall clear the path.
4. There is a way through every block.
5. Understand through compassion or you will misunderstand the times.

These five sutras I came to learn through Kundalini Yoga, held me through the growth processes as part of the dissolution of my marriage. When we are allowing instead of fighting, the Hague Convention has to shift to align with the natural attraction point of lovingness. It is with deep intention to co-create a more flowing reality for international families that this book is birthed.

May it nourish the dialogue towards healing rather

than winning, towards helping rather than condemning, towards empowerment rather than victimhood, towards acceptance rather than denial, and towards belonging rather than ostracising.

May all the components needed for emergence find each other and come together easily so that the convergence process is lovingly held to fulfil its catalytic mission.

As Nancy said before, our work is to take the pearl and move forward, changed; we are not our traumas, and we are not the same person today as we were then.

Love with passion and perspective.

Bring forth that healthful flowing balance to the tone of movement throughout life.

I leave you with the song We All Know The Truth by Banco de Gaia (https://www.youtube.com/watch?v=-NiY7m3rpNs).

May it nourish you in the many ways you so wish to be nourished.

ADDITIONAL RESOURCES

GENERAL

Adams, Kenneth. Silently Seduced: When Parents Make Their Children Partners - Understanding Covert Incest. Health Communications, 1992.

Behary, Wendy. Disarming the Narcissist. New Harbinger Publications. 2013.

Craven, Pat. Living With The Dominator: A book about the Freedom Programme. Freedom Publishing. 2008.

Forward, Susan. Men Who Hate Women and The Women Who Love Them. Bantam Books. 1986.

Hellinger, Bert. Acknowledging What Is. Zeig, Tucker & Co., 1999.

Hellinger, Bert. Love's Hidden Symmetry. Zeig, Tucker & Co., 1998.

Hicks, Esther and Jerry. The Vortex. Hay House, US. 2009.

Lim, Adele M. Live Your Whole Capacity: How to tap into and grow unknown potential in your life. I_AM Self Publishing, UK. 2017.

McGraw, Phil. Life Code. Bird Street Books, US. 2012.

Peabody, Susan. Addiction to Love - Overcoming Obsession and Dependency in Relationships. Celestial Arts, Crown Publishing Group, 2005.

Richo, David. How to be an Adult in Relationships. Shambala. 2002.

Swithin, Tina. Divorcing a Narcissist: Advice from the Battlefield. Tina Swithin. 2014.

Welwood, John. Journey of the Heart - The Path of Conscious Love. Harper, 1990.

Whitfield, Charles. Healing the Child Within. Health Communications. 1989.

Wilson Schaff, Anne. Escape From Intimacy. Harper One. 1986.

Saeed, Kim
https://letmereach.com/

https://www.youtube.com/watch?v=nPBBGb-p0S0

https://www.youtube.com/watch?v=vEJFsg0net8

Evans, Melanie Tonia
https://blog.melanietoniaevans.com/shifts-happen-healing-the-traumas-closest-to-our-hearts-our-children-2/

Miller, Meredith
https://innerintegration.mykajabi.com/

https://youtu.be/rzpX2Ozt7tc

https://www.youtube.com/watch?v=x0bZy1eOPlw

Cole, Terri
https://www.youtube.com/watch?v=Fp1auZKZQHs

PARENTS AND CHILDREN

Purple Mother, Blue Father
https://www.youtube.com/watch?v=XoQ3_UebI3I

https://www.amazon.com/When-Parents-Divorce-Father-Purple-ebook/dp/B0064AILWO

Sun, Moon, Daughter
http://www.sunmoondaughter.com

Fred Stays With Me
https://www.amazon.com/Fred-Stays-Me-Nancy-Coffelt/dp/0316077917

https://www.youtube.com/watch?v=ZPR4mUZ59K8

Two Homes
https://www.amazon.com/Two-Homes-Claire-Masurel/dp/0763619841

The Family Book
https://www.youtube.com/watch?v=MIm_H01Z6Ss

https://www.amazon.com/Family-Book-Todd-Parr/dp/0316070408

Who's in a Family
https://www.amazon.com/Whos-Family-Robert-Skutch/dp/188367266X

No Means No!: Teaching children about personal boundaries, respect and consent; empowering kids by respecting their choices and their right to say, 'No!'
https://www.amazon.com/No-Means-boundaries-empowering-respecting/dp/1925089223

Some Secrets Should Never Be Kept
https://www.amazon.com/Some-Secrets-Should-Never-Kept/

dp/0987186019
Huge Bag of Worries
https://www.youtube.com/watch?v=G4obF25b6Fc

https://www.amazon.com/Huge-Bag-Worries-Virginia-Ironside/dp/0340903171

Let's Talk PANTS
https://www.nspcc.org.uk/preventing-abuse/keeping-children-safe/underwear-rule/

Bryson, Tina Payne and Siegel, Daniel. The Whole-Brain Child – 12 Proven Strategies to Nurture Your Child's Developing Mind. New York: Bantam Books, 2012.

Dancy, Rahima Baldwin. You Are Your Child's First Teacher. New York: Random House, 2012.

Payne, Kim John and Ross, Lisa M. Simplicity Parenting – Using the Extraordinary Power of Less to Raise Calmer, Happier, and More Secure Kids. New York: Random House, 2010.

Perrow, Susan. Healing Stories for Challenging Behaviour. Gloucester: Hawthorn Press, 2008.

ABOUT THE AUTHOR

Adele M Lim is the Founder of and Lead Catalyst at Whole Capacity, a global web of catalysts working with individuals and organisations to facilitate movement and innovation in change and growth. With an emphasis on systemic approaches and leading from the core, her work inspires and sustains change on multiple levels. Her application of individual and organisation development practices are grounded in a practical understanding of how things are on the ground.

An author of personal development and children's books, she brings to her clients a lifetime's journey including extensive training and experience in family dynamics, leadership coaching, talent management and organisation development. She has served as an internal and external consultant to blue chip multinationals in a variety of sectors across global environments.

Adele is the creator of Lovingspace, a project series in support of international families experiencing massive change, following a complicated cross-border divorce and meeting with the Hague Abduction Convention, a multilateral treaty developed by the Hague Conference on Private International Law (HCCH), drafted in 1980 to ensure prompt return of children to their country of habitual residence if found to have been wrongfully retained in another contracting state.

Through children's books, women's circle and online broadcasts, Lovingspace hopes to communicate the sanctity of the family despite the personalities that play alongside structural and geographical differences, the orders of today's global village. It weaves in the emergence via collective alignment with the energy of love and well-being that comes through the convergence of resonant groups.

Adele holds an MSc in Information Management and Finance from University of Westminster, and a Certificate in Organisation Development from NTL Institute (formerly National Training Laboratories of Bethel, Maine). Her professional training includes Systemic Constellations, Theory U, and the Inner Dance Energy School. She is also a Chartered Member of the CIPD, UK, and the Founder of Rawfully Whole, an integrative, cooperative platform that supports women in enabling the living of their deepest truth and passion.

For more information, visit:

http://wholecapacity.com
http://facebook.com/wholecapacity
http://rawfullywhole.com
http://facebook.com/rawfullywhole
http://facebook.com/groups/passionsharefest